ABOUT EDUCARING, THE RIE™ APPROACH

Infant specialist MAGDA GERBER says:

"If we could observe and see infants as completely competent for the stage at which they are, we would learn from and about them, rather than teach them. Being around infants reminds us how to, be 'real,' 'genuine,' 'authentic.' "

"When we help a child feel secure, feel appreciated, feel that 'somebody is deeply, truly interested in me,' by the way we just look, the way we just listen, we influence a child's whole personality, the way that child sees life."

A CENTER DIRECTOR says:

"As a manager, I have been able to incorporate RIE's principles into our infant/toddler program and also into my own management style. Our center has been successful in developing teams that work together and feel appreciated by their peers."

PARENTS say:

"RIE is not dogmatic; it is as flexible as each person's own inner voice.... There's nothing to buy; it's a matter of seeing and hearing what's right before our eyes."

"RIE has a commonsense simplicity that allows everyone in the family to be heard and respected."

"RIE has strengthened our ability to learn directly from our daughter about her needs, interests and competencies."

A CAREGIVER says:

"RIE helped me to support parents and their infants by relaxing, trusting, and tuning in to the needs of the infant and the concerns of the parent. It helped me respect myself and accept that this work is a lifelong process of awareness and reflection."

A PARENT-INFANT TEACHER says:

"My work has become easier, more interesting, and more satisfying."

DEAR PARENT

CARING FOR INFANTS WITH RESPECT

Expanded Edition

MAGDA GERBER

Edited by Joan Weaver

A publication of Resources for Infant Educarers (RIE™)
Los Angeles, California

DEAR PARENT CARING FOR INFANTS WITH RESPECT
Expanded Edition
by Magda Gerber, edited by Joan Weaver
Additional chapters on Family Child Care and Center-Based Care

Published by: Resources for Infant Educarers (RIE™)

1550 Murray Circle
Los Angeles, CA 90026
(323) 663-5330, FAX (323) 663-5586
website: www.RIE.org, email: Educarer@RIE.org

Copyright © 1998, 2002 by Magda Gerber
Publication coordinated by Ruth R. Money,
with Elizabeth Memel, Carol Pinto, and Bill Josephs.
Photos by Karen Ziskin.
Cover Design by Kristen Dietrick.

Additional Chapter 48 by Ruth R. Money, Chapter 49 by Catherine Coughlan.
Additional photos by Denise Kelton (pages 4 & 32), Melody Lawrence (pages 14 & 48),
Jung Sun Wohn (page 89), Jude Keith Rose (page 122), Daisy Gerber (pages 128 &
202), Jody Perlman (page 150), Nina Arthur (pages 192, 201, 211 & 212); unknown
photographer (inside front cover).

Printed in the United States of America on acid-free paper.

Cataloging-in-Publication Data provided by Publisher
Gerber, Magda
    Dear parent : caring for infants with respect / [written by] Magda Gerber ; edited
by Joan Weaver. Expanded ed., 2nd ed. — Los Angeles, CA : Resources for Infant
Educarers (RIE™), 2002.
    xviii, 223 p. : ill. ; 23 cm.
    Title from spine: Caring for infants with respect.
    Includes two new chapters: A brief visit to a RIE infant center by Ruth R. Money ;
RIE in a family child care home by Catherine Coughlan.
    Includes index.
    ISBN 10: 1-892560-06-2   ISBN 13: 978-1-892560-06-3
    1. Infants — Care. 2. Parenting. 3. Child care. 4. Child rearing. 5. Caregivers —
Training of. 6. Day care centers. 7. Family day care. I. Money, Ruth R. II. Coughlan,
Catherine. III. Weaver, Joan. IV. Resources for Infant Educarers (RIE™). V. RIE™. VI.
Title. VII. Title: Caring for infants with respect.
    HQ744.G47 2002
    649'.122—dc21

MIX
Paper from
responsible sources
FSC® C011935

To the worldwide RIE and Pikler communities,
supporting wellness from the very beginning of life,

and

to parents and professionals everywhere,
may you be guided and inspired by the infants
in your care.

Although the ideas in this book have worked for many families, not all suggestions may be suitable for you and your child. The author and publisher advise you to use your common sense and your intimate knowledge of your own child. We cannot be held responsible for the misuse of any information in this book.

Contents

Preface to the
Second Edition

THIS EDITION HAS BEEN EXPANDED to include two new chapters on using RIE principles to care for infants in group settings. Although the situation in an infant day care center or family day care home is different from that within the family, the philosophy and even the methods are the same: each infant is given personalized, one-to-one care.

In the main chapters of the book, Magda Gerber explains in great detail how to care for an infant respectfully, focusing on the establishment of an authentic, trusting relationship between the adult and infant. This interaction between mother and baby, based on observation and reciprocal responsiveness, is the model for others who want to provide respectful one-to-one care for infants in groups. Respectful relationships among caregivers, parents, and administrators are also integral to the success of a child care center. Four chapters of the Appendix address the topic of caring for infants in various group settings.

When the idea of individual care in a group situation is proposed, the question is often asked, "What do you do when all four infants are crying to be fed at the same time?" This book shows infants in group care settings enjoying individual care rather than assembly-line treatment. It shows infants adjusting to a predictable rhythm where the infants know that they will each have an unhurried turn when their physical needs will be met by feeding, changing, or holding; and their emotional needs will be met by the Educarer's individualized quality of attention.

As more and more mothers with young children have entered the work force in recent years, RIE has been actively dedicated to improving the quality of infant care in centers and other settings. This effort has been spurred on by research showing that secure attachment to one person is good, but to two is better, and by another study of infants in day care showing the importance of secure attachment to the other primary caregivers in addition to the parents. It is in the security of the relationship that the infant finds the freedom to develop optimally and to learn about the world.

The development of guidelines for putting RIE principles of Educaring into practice in infant care centers began with the founding of the first RIE demonstration infant care center in 1988. Other centers continue to use these guidelines today as part of RIE's accreditation process.

With the addition of these new chapters on group care and education, we hope that the book will open insights on how it is possible and practical to care for infants in an unhurried, one-to-one respectful way in a group setting. Caregivers who model and share this approach with parents can be a support to parents in their important job of establishing a lifelong relationship with their children starting in infancy.

RUTH R. MONEY

Acknowledgments
From the First Edition

FOR MANY DECADES, my work has focused on infants from birth until two years of age. Throughout my tenure as director of Resources for Infant Educarers, and previously with the Demonstration Infant Program, I have been surrounded by dedicated and hardworking volunteers. In the preparation of this book, I would like to thank:

All the parents who shared their experiences and those involved in publishing RIE's quarterly newsletter, *Educaring*, where much of the material first appeared (and especially Lisa Bailey, Tinker Beatty, Deborah Bellini, Valorie Cole, Prosy Delacruz, Jill Flyer, Linda Hinrichs, Becky Hopkins, Andrea King, Peter Mangione, Lelia Moskowitz, Maria Papacostaki, Carol Pinto, Julia Poll, Mimi Sabo, Ellen Sandler, Isabel Story, Joyce Taylor and Noreen Winkler, whose anecdotes are quoted herein, in italics);

Joan Weaver, my editor, whose vision, determination and organization made this book a reality;

Ruth Money, who assumed the responsibility, with RIE, for publishing and distributing this first edition of *Dear Parent*;

Carol Pinto and Elizabeth Memel, who with Joan and Ruth worked as a team throughout the design, review, and publication process;

Bill Josephs, who did the desktop publishing;

Karen Ziskin, Melody Lawrence, Jude Keith Rose, Jung Sun Wohn, Jody Pearlman, Coleen McClure Morell, Denise Kelton and Daisy Gerber, who took the photographs;

Hari Grebler and David Wakeam, who designed the front cover;

All those who commented on the manuscript in its various stages, especially Kei Kaneshiro, Linda Hinrichs and Zina Josephs;

All those who contributed additional expertise in the technical and practical aspects of the book's publication and distribution (and especially Ed and Irene Van der Zande and the staff at the Santa Cruz Toddler Care Center, whose book based on the RIE philosophy, *1, 2, 3... The Toddler Years*, focuses on life with older infants);

My other friends and colleagues for their many years of dedicated support;

My children: Mayo, Daisy and Bence.

MAGDA GERBER

And from the Editor:

Special thanks to my RIE colleagues Ruth Money, Elizabeth Memel and Carol Pinto, and to Bill Josephs and Kei Kaneshiro for all their efforts; to Sandy Davie of the Santa Cruz Toddler Care Center and Diana Suskind, who listened and encouraged; to Robert Mann, who first told me about Magda; and to my three families (Weaver, Drulias, Groell), to Magda Gerber and to Lucinda Ziesing for their unique and important contributions to my personal and professional growth along the way.

JOAN WEAVER

Author's Note

I STILL REMEMBER MY first reaction after the birth of my daughter. I was amazed at how difficult it was to be a parent. I was angry. Why didn't anyone prepare me for this? I thought I was the only one who didn't know what to do with babies and somehow in my education someone had forgotten to tell me. Does this sound familiar to you?

Parenting is a most difficult job for which you cannot really prepare yourself. Can we make it easier? My answer is yes!

How?—by not trying to do the impossible while missing the obvious.

Enjoy More, Work Less

At RIE we urge parents to relax, observe, and enjoy what their babies *are* doing, noticing and enjoying new skills as they develop naturally.

A parent's role is to provide a secure and predictable environment. You do have to be sensitive to your infant's changing needs; the infant has to feel your caring presence. But you don't have to teach. You don't have to buy more gadgets. You and your infant can just exist and enjoy each other as your relationship develops.

The misleading thing about this is that it sounds so easy. But it isn't, because in our society we are bombarded with messages to buy this and teach that.

No matter how impressive any philosophy of child rearing may sound, it is quite another to apply it to everyday situations.

It is difficult to believe that one can be a better parent by sitting and watching. Yet, our motto is, "Observe more, do less." In asking parents to accept this different mode of parenting, we are asking a lot.

In giving parents advice, I apply principles used by Dr. Emmi Pikler along with those I have developed for babies; I make information available, and parents use it when they are ready for it (See, *Reflections on My Work with Dr. Pikler,* page 185). I do present my knowledge and experiences, hoping that eventually you will try to implement some of these ideas and that you will keep trying even if the new approach does not bring miraculous results right away (although sometimes it does).

Understanding, Insight, Long-Term Learning

At RIE we like to "sow seeds." We offer guidelines for sorting through the many conflicting and confusing bits of advice that will come your way as parents; what it will be like living with a new baby; how to prepare the physical environment; what to buy, and certainly what not to buy. We discuss what to expect from a newborn and a young baby and how to do the impossible: respond to a newborn's needs without completely exhausting yourselves. We focus on how to develop a dialogue, how to respond to a crying baby, your role, the baby's role, etc. We help parents understand how a baby learns to trust, how he develops skills and competencies, and how to learn about each baby's unique characteristics. We talk about how to let your infant know about your expectations, and just what those expectations are, both overt and covert. In summary, we plant "confident parent seeds."

My goal is for you really to understand what I mean. Then you can take what you like and reject what you don't like. But that is what is so difficult, the understanding.

It is easy to give advice, but if good advice would work, we would all be perfect. I do not expect you or any other parent to be superhuman. I just hope that the RIE principles will slowly become part of your awareness, your thinking and your actions, and that eventually, when they truly become part of you, they will serve you as your own inner guidelines. Those inner guidelines can gently remind you whenever you slip to "try again," which means to use a little more patience, empathy, and sensitivity next time.

What we are trying to impart is a quality of experience—a way of relating that can be used at all levels of growth. In the long run our goal is to help parents learn to live and let live with their infants and later with their older children. Such insight cannot be "taught." Long-term learning is a slow process. It must happen organically—allowing for time in which the seeds of understanding may sprout, grow, bloom, and bear fruit.

And especially for expectant parents, I would like to add: I am aware that now you are preoccupied with the birth of your baby, and everything that happens afterwards may seem remote and intangible. Yet this is the ideal time to become acquainted with some basic RIE ideas. If you were to ask parents who learned about the RIE approach later, they would tell you how much easier it is to develop good habits from the beginning than to undo and change "bad" habits later.

Seeing Infants With New Eyes

While there are many organizations, classes, and publications which desire to improve the care of infants, we believe there is a difference in the way we at RIE see the infant.

I hope that parents, reading this book, will appreciate the

difference if they observe the way infants develop and learn when they are allowed to move at their own time and in their own way. I hope that parents will let go of the belief that, unless they help or teach them, their infants will not learn motor skills soon enough or well enough. I hope parents will learn to relax and observe their babies and enjoy seeing new miracles happening all of the time. I hope children will grow up with less anxiety, more confidence and more security.

If some of this anxiety, anger and frustration could be eliminated, could it possibly affect our anxious and angry society? Let us hope so!

Good luck and many rewards.

1. EDUCARING: Meeting the Needs of Infants and Parents

W HAT DO INFANTS really need, and how can parents recognize and meet those needs? Also, what do parents need, and how can they recognize and meet their own needs?

Becoming acquainted with some basic RIE ideas can make your incredibly difficult task as a parent much easier and more pleasurable. The RIE approach is surprisingly simple and commonsensical. (RIE is pronounced "rye.")

We should educate while we care and care while we educate.

To emphasize this, I coined the words "Educarer" and "Educaring" to describe our philosophy.

The Basis of the RIE Approach: RESPECT

Respect is the basis of the RIE philosophy.

We not only respect babies, we demonstrate our respect every time we interact with them. Respecting a child means treating even the youngest infant as a unique human being, not as an object.

At RIE we show respect, for example, by not picking up an infant without telling him beforehand, by talking directly to him and not over him, and by waiting for the child's response. Such respectful attitudes help to develop an authentic child.

1

Our Goal: An Authentic Child

An authentic child is one who feels secure, autonomous, and competent.

When we help a child to feel secure, feel appreciated, feel that "somebody is deeply, truly interested in me," by the way we just look, the way we just listen, we influence that child's whole personality, the way that child sees life.

Trust in the Infant's Competence

We have basic trust in the infant to be an initiator, to be an explorer eager to learn what he is ready for.

Because of this trust, we provide the infant with only enough help necessary to allow the child to enjoy mastery of her own actions.

Sensitive Observation

Our method, guided by respect for the infant's competence, is observation. We observe carefully to understand the infant's communications and his needs.

The more we observe, the more we understand and appreciate the enormous amount and speed of learning that happens during the first two or three years of life. We become more humble, we teach less, and we provide an environment for learning instead.

Caregiving Times: Involving the Child

During care activities (diapering, feeding, bathing, dressing, etc.), we encourage even the tiniest infant to become an active participant rather than a passive recipient of the activities. Parents create opportunities for interaction, cooperation, intimacy and mutual enjoyment by being wholeheartedly with the infant during the time they spend together anyway.

"Refueled" by such unhurried, pleasurable caring experiences, infants are ready to explore their environment with only minimal intervention by adults.

A Safe, Challenging, Predictable Environment

Our role is to create an environment in which the child can best do all the things that the child would do naturally. The more predictable an environment is, the easier it is for babies to learn.

As infants become more mobile, they need safe, appropriate space in which to move. Their natural, inborn desire to move should not be handicapped by the environment.

Time for Uninterrupted Play and Freedom to Explore

We give the infant plenty of time for uninterrupted play. Instead of trying to teach babies new skills while they play and explore, we appreciate and admire what babies are actually doing.

Consistency

We establish clearly defined limits and communicate our expectations to develop discipline.

EDUCARING: A Secure Beginning

At RIE, parents learn how infant and family rhythms develop into predictable routines and how "separate time" and "together time" can be enjoyed.

If you identify and agree with our basic principles, you can use them to develop inner guidelines for responding to the many perplexing issues of parenthood.

2. Caregiving Routines: One-to-One, with Full Attention

WHAT AN INFANT NEEDS—what every human being wants—is to experience the full *undivided attention* of a parent or other significant person. But nobody can pay full attention all of the time.

The natural time to be wholeheartedly with your child is the time you do spend together anyway—while you *care* for your baby. Think of these "taking-care-of" routines as very special, the "refueling" time for both of you—time for intimate togetherness.

Take the telephone off the hook before you intend to feed, bathe, or diaper your baby, and tell your infant, "I'm going to take the phone off the hook so nobody will disturb us, because now I really want to be just with you." (When you say it, you reinforce yourself.)

"Unbusy" your head and "unbusy" your body. Be fully there, interested only in your baby for that time.

I believe it is healthy for any child to get this genuine interest.

Approaching caregiving as quality time with your infant will give you more enjoyable time together, and will give him the feeling that you value your time together, which affirms for your infant his value as a person. After such intimate moments, your baby will be pleased to explore by himself if you have prepared the proper environment. (See, *Time Apart: A Space for Your Baby*, page 15)

The following guidelines are designed for making all care activities enjoyable, quality times, rich with invaluable learning experiences.

- *Prepare ahead.* Before involving the baby, have everything ready so you won't have to search for a diaper, spoon, towel or an item of clothing, which would disrupt the continuity of your time together.

- *Observe what the child is doing.* If he is absorbed in activity, do not interrupt him, but wait for the right moment to intervene.

- *Explain to your child what you are going to do.* This pattern can begin in early infancy in all interactions. Although the infant does not understand your words at first, he will soon begin to associate your sounds and tone of voice with your gestures and actions, and his anticipation will grow for enjoyable time shared together with his parents.

- *Communicate with the child.* Once you have the infant's attention, tell him you want to do something together. Gently take any toys or objects out of his hands, explaining what you are doing, and *tell him you want to pick him up now.* Reach out and wait for a response. Do not pick up your child unexpectedly or from behind. Begin this pattern even with very young infants, who may not show any visible response at first. It helps foster a style of two-way communication that respectfully involves the child.

- *Explain and show your infant what you are doing, step by step.* Allow your infant to follow and

6

become involved in the process, to make eye contact, study your face, vocalize, initiate play, follow your actions and respond to you, and you to him.

- *Slow down.* In order for your baby to have time to truly participate, everything you do should be "slowed down."

- *Pay full attention.* Whenever you care, do it absolutely with full attention. If you pay half attention all the time, that's never full attention. Babies are then always half hungry for attention. But if you pay full attention part of the time, then you go a long way. That's what I would recommend: to be fully with a child and then let him be.

These guidelines are general, and you will find that, as your infant matures, you will need to continually adapt to your child's age and stage of development. You will need to get a "feel" for your own style of interaction, sensitive to the distinct personalities of each of you. The social interactions of the infant and parent are full of the unexpected, full of new delights and new challenges.

From the very beginning, we have tried to let Julia know what we are going to do with her before doing it. Although we believed in relating to Julia with respect, we did not anticipate the power of this type of communication. We quickly learned that words were not our only means of communicating to Julia about what was coming next. A knock on her door, a touch on her hand or foot, eye contact, or the movement of our hands conveyed a message to Julia. If the message came slowly, and promptly preceded an action, she started to anticipate our next movement or action.

Julia's responsiveness to our communications would not be possible without giving her time to respond. We were both determined to follow Magda's advice to slow down with Julia, but at first, we did not realize how slow "slow" should be. Even when we thought we were going slowly, Julia sometimes would look a little out of sorts. If we would make our "slow pace" slower, she would calm down and become alert.

The impact of respectful communication became most apparent during routines. When we would change Julia's clothes, for instance, we would be deliberate and let her know about each action. Before slipping her arm through a sleeve, we would touch her and say to her in simple words what was going to happen. During the first several weeks, she looked to the side when her clothes were changed, but she nevertheless seemed to be paying attention. Then, she started to look at us during clothes changes and observed each of our actions.

Soon she started participating in little ways. She would pull up on an arm when it was time to slip it out of a sleeve. Julia's growing interest and involvement in changing time made it one of the most enjoyable times with her. Even when she was fussy, she would calm down and become alert when one of us would take her to the changing table. Her grandmother, who saw Julia for the first time at nine weeks, commented that she had never seen a baby take such delight at changing time. In fact, one time when Julia was quite upset, her grandmother jokingly suggested that we do a changing routine to help Julia settle down. Sure enough, as soon as one of us let Julia know that we were going to take her to the changing table, she became calm and alert.

Respectful communication has also added to the pleasure of nursing for her mother, Mimi. When the time would come for switching sides, Mimi would consistently say to Julia that she was going to break Julia's suction on the breast, wait for several moments, and then with her finger gently touch Julia's lip. After a few weeks, Julia started to pull away from the breast on her own when Mimi would say to Julia it was time to change sides.

The framework I have set forth is open enough to allow space within its structure for you to be able to grow with your child, to improvise and respond spontaneously to unexpected behaviors, and to stay cued in and aware of your child as an individual. This "personalized" approach to caregiving promotes the development of an infant's self-confidence, body awareness, social attentiveness and responsiveness. It also encourages an infant in the difficult, but crucial and exciting, struggle for autonomy.

An infant who is allowed to participate actively in the process of his care will be encouraged to be a willingly independent child and to master his own self-care as he grows older.

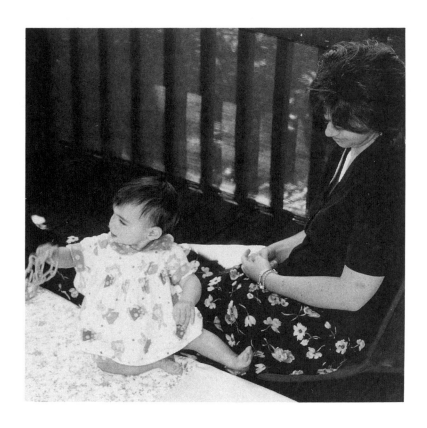

3. On Teaching and Learning

A<small>N</small> INFANT always learns. At RIE we believe that babies should not be taught because it usually interferes with learning. The less we interfere with the natural process of learning, the more we can observe how much infants learn all the time.

Infants constantly learn by taking in, finding out, discovering, integrating and organizing the real world around them. Knowledge gained this way will serve them best in their everyday lives.

If only people would trust nature's plan for how babies are created, they could relax and enjoy all the daily miracles of natural development.

What to Teach? Why?

Parents are the first and the most important teachers of their children. I also know how pressured parents are by books, articles, television and by other parents to *do* something to stimulate learning in their infants. (See, *Fads and Trends in Child Rearing*, page 151)

We believe that infants always do what they can do, what they want to do, what they are compelled from inside to do. How do adults dare believe they know what an infant is ready to learn at any particular moment?

Most people teach what infants know or would learn anyway. Don't average, normal children in average, "good enough" environments learn about colors, about shapes, about off and on?

11

Why teach it, when they learn these concepts so well in an everyday environment with an attentive parent? I think Jean Piaget said it beautifully: When you teach a child something, you take away forever his chance of discovering it for himself.

Whenever you restrict an infant from doing what he could and would do naturally, in my mind you tell the child, "I know what's good for you." But you, the adult, do not know. For example, most children (not all), when they first go down stairs, go head first—they like to see where they go. Some people say it's safer for infants to crawl down stairs backwards, and they teach infants how to go down in that way. The child may become confused because his body tells him one thing and the adult another, and then the child may fall.

The way a baby moves naturally, when he does what feels right for his body at that particular time, is always the safest. (See, *At Their Own Time, and In Their Own Way*, page 53)

If you teach something a child is not ready for, that child may feel, "I don't quite know what is expected of me, but whatever I do is not appreciated."

I wonder if parents realize that taking time to teach their infant may deprive the infant of time spent learning what *is* relevant.

Free Movement, Free Play

We do not teach infants how to move, because we believe each baby knows much better. We do not interfere with their play. We do not interfere with what they choose from the available materials. These are areas where at RIE we say, absolutely, "hands off." We are always interested to know, "What would this child choose to do now, if not taught to do something else?"

Young children are explorers and initiators. They learn in

spite of what we teach. A safe environment in which the baby can move and explore provides the kind of learning experience the child profits from the most. When infants have enough space, safe space, they will do exactly the movements that they are ready for—because they have the opportunity.

As we observe infants, it almost looks as if they are working rather than playing: they are fully involved, absorbed in what they are doing. We don't need to invent exercises for them. They learn to follow their instincts and to trust their own judgment.

Infants accomplish mastery by endless repetitions, continuing the same activity over and over again, long after adults may have lost interest. When an infant repeats an action many, many times, he is not bored. Rather, he is learning thoroughly about that action, making it a part of himself and his world. When he has learned it to his own satisfaction, he will move on to another new activity.

While playing, children work through conflicts with objects, other children and adults. Play provides an outlet for curiosity, information about the physical world, and a safe way to deal with anxiety and social relationships. In the long run, play serves children's inner needs, hopes and aspirations.

Learning About Everyday Life

What should infants really learn from their parents? When the parents tell the child what they are doing, the baby learns about the real world around him. Babies have to learn the most important things in life—who they are, how to communicate, what makes mommy or daddy happy or upset. Teaching is not a separate function. It is an everyday life experience. The best thing to teach a young baby is everyday life.

- About his needs: "You seem thirsty. Would you like

this drink?"

- About his belongings: "Let's put your shirt on. Are you ready to put your arm in the sleeve?"
- About your concerns: "The street isn't safe. I cannot let you run after your ball."

What parents teach is themselves, as models of what is human—by their moods, their reactions, their facial expressions and actions. These are the real things parents need to be aware of, and of how they affect their children. Allow them to know you, and it might become easier for them to learn about themselves.

4. Time Apart: A Space for Your Baby

EVERY INFANT NEEDS an absolutely safe environment, one in which he can freely move around as his motor skills develop.

A safe environment not only allows the infant to spend uninterrupted time exploring and learning, but also allows the parents to pursue their own projects. When the child needs care again, both infant and parents can enjoy the interaction fully without distraction.

(My definition of a safe environment is this: if whoever is in charge of the infant were someday accidentally locked out of the house until the end of the day, the infant would survive. The infant might be upset, be tired, be hungry, be crying—but the infant would still be safe.)

A Peaceful Environment

Frequently young babies are subjected to too much stimulation. Often adults do not recognize an infant's need for peace and quiet.

Many times the appropriate place for your baby is his own space or own room. He should be within hearing distance of the parent, but out of the way of too much household activity.

Some experts tell you to take your baby with you wherever you go to give her security. We believe that babies derive security not only from being near their parents but also from being allowed to explore their environment freely on their own.

(See, *Time Together, Time Apart*, page 17)

You need to check in frequently and, of course, be available when the baby needs to be fed, diapered, bathed, etc. By all means, be with your baby when you enjoy relaxing and just watching him. (See, *Quality Time*, page 75)

From Crib to Playpen to Floor

A bassinet or crib is all right to start, and a playpen is suitable until the baby starts turning over and moving about by rolling. In the first months infants are not locomotive—cannot move far away from where we put them—so they do not find these small places restrictive. On the contrary, it is their familiar place with their familiar objects in it. Boundaries give these babies feelings of security.

With a duplicate crib and a playpen out-of-doors, a baby can spend many hours napping and playing in a safe place outside without parents having to watch every minute. (See, *Outdoor Living*, page 103)

At about five to six months, as your baby becomes more mobile, she can spend increasingly more time on the floor in her larger safe space. Having some simple objects near enough for her to be able to reach will allow her to manipulate them and play. Having some objects just out of reach may encourage her to move towards them.

First "Toys"

For the first two months, babies' most valuable play objects are their own hands and their parents' faces, etc.

As a first "toy," I recommend a scarf about 18 inches square, made of strong, colorful cotton, such as Dr. Pikler used at Loczy. (Silk or nylon is dangerous, as is a scarf that is too small.) Hold the scarf in the middle and place it to make a peak. This will provide an interesting visual target. The reason I prefer the scarf over mobiles is that, when the infant is ready, she will be able to grasp and manipulate this material in endless ways, always having new sights and feelings: pulling it over, then on, her face; chewing on it; lying on it, not being able to pull it out from under her own body; or later, tugging it back and forth with another infant. (See, *Choosing Play Objects*, page 97)

Safe Boundaries

Before your child starts rolling and crawling is the best time to child-proof a room, using a gate to prevent his going into unsafe territory. (If a whole room is not available, part of a room can safely be partitioned.)

Parents often react negatively when I suggest using gates in the home to create boundaries for their infants. Contrary to what many people believe, a gated room is a safe room which gives infants *freedom* to move and explore in safe and familiar surroundings. If the gate has been part of your baby's environment from the beginning, he will naturally accept it just like any other familiar object surrounding him. If, on the other hand, you put it up *after* he has crept out of his room, he will rightly view it as a restraining device to keep him from doing what he wants.

How much better it is, in my opinion, to create a truly safe place, with a secure gate to divide it from the rest of the house, than to keep a child "safe" by either strapping him into a swing, infant seat, etc., or by constantly following him around in order to restrain him from household hazards.

Time Together, Time Apart

When adults try to do their own work while trying to pay

attention to their children, both parent and child end up feeling frustrated. This trap, I feel, is created by books and advisors who say that a baby needs to have his parent near him at all times. As a result, many parents move their babies around with them, placing them on kitchen tables, bathroom floors and other unsafe places. A confined baby, strapped in an infant seat, is limited in his movement and has less freedom than a child actively exploring his own familiar space behind a safety gate.

Children learn best through involvement, both with their environment and with others. If a child has a pleasant place to play, where he can move around on his own, exploring his environment, this, in turn, frees the parents to do their own work, and both their needs and their child's needs can be met.

Many parents are concerned about not being "good parents" when they are not with their child. I still do not quite understand why it is so difficult for parents to accept that it is all right to leave a child in this totally safe space, while the parent is available but doing something else within hearing distance. (See, *One Family, One Saturday*, page 173)

A baby can learn to spend time by himself. It is important for him to discover satisfaction and joy in his own independence. Children who have learned to rely on being stimulated, manipulated and entertained by adults may lose their capacities to be absorbed in independent, exploratory activities.

Infants don't need constant attention—what they need is to be safe and secure. Certainly being shuffled from room to room while the parent works does not build security.

An adult way of life is not a child's way of life. Both parents and infants need time for themselves. Spending time apart helps make the together times all the more rich.

5. Allowing Infants to Do What They Can Do

IT IS UNDERSTANDABLE that new parents believe that, if they can raise their children well, their children will live happily ever after. In spite of "knowing better," parents dream of recreating "paradise" where their children never hurt or suffer or even have to struggle.

This desire makes parents provide constant entertainment, allow no frustration, and continually carry their baby around all the time. They may even feed their baby after the first whimper, without waiting to find out if the baby is really hungry. Is this a way to prepare for real life? On the other hand, can we expect a young baby to be able to cope with the many ongoing frustrations of daily life? How can a parent keep a balance between over-indulgence and not helping enough?

The reality of human life is that every child has to eventually separate and become her own person. This is a gradual process. Parental attitudes can make it easier or more difficult. To accept and enjoy the present, at every developmental stage, makes it easy. To try to push or interfere with natural development makes it difficult.

19

"Observe, and Wait"

The role of a parent is to continuously assess whether the infant is capable of handling a situation. For instance, when an infant looks at an object (or maybe even reaches for it), many adults rush to hand the object to the infant—not realizing that, by doing so, they deprive the infant of acting spontaneously and learning from his own actions.

As I say so often, "Observe, and wait." Sometimes you may even find out that what you believed the infant wanted was only your assumption. It is natural to make mistakes and easy to misunderstand pre-verbal children. Nevertheless, it is important to keep trying.

Infancy is a time of great dependence. However, babies should be allowed to do some things for themselves from the very beginning.

Here are some other examples of what I mean:

- Mother places her nipple on baby's cheek. The rooting reflex moves baby's head towards the breast.
- Father, with outstretched arms, looks at baby and asks, "Do you want to be picked up?" Baby is given time to make a choice.
- An eleven-month-old's ball gets stuck under a shelf. His expression shows he is upset. He kicks his legs. Parent says, "Oh, your ball got stuck. What can you do?" Child cries. Parent waits quietly or may say, "This upsets you," showing empathy without taking over. Child pulls ball and ball rolls out.

Had the mother thrust the breast into the baby's mouth, had the father picked up the baby regardless of the baby's reaction, or had the parent given the ball to the child, these children could have been deprived of trying to handle the situation, learning by doing, and experiencing the joy of mastery.

Trust your baby's competence. She wants to do things for herself, and she can do things for herself.

You also know that sometimes your infant does need help, but try to provide just that little amount of help that allows the child to take over again. Let her be the initiator and problem-solver.

We can look at life as a continuation of conflicts or problems. The more often we have mastered a minute difficulty, the more capable we feel the next time.

Competent and Confident

By closely supervising our infants, by allowing them to do what they are capable of, by restraining ourselves from rescuing them too often, by waiting and waiting and waiting, by giving minimal help when they really need it, we allow our infants to learn and grow at their own time, and in their own way.

I believe that, no matter how much and how fast the world changes, a well-grounded, competent and confident person is best equipped to adapt to it. This is our goal.

Magda asked us to observe the babies to see what they chose to do on their own. This wasn't easy for me. I could not sit back and allow Rachel the least frustration or difficulty. I was too anxious to sit quietly and allow Rachel to cry and struggle. When she cried, I felt uneasy and wanted to do anything to stop the crying. Magda asked if I could make myself wait before I intervened. As I was waiting to see if Rachel could handle things on her own, I realized that inside my grown-up self there was a restless, helpless child who did not know what to do. I still wonder about

21

the source of this restlessness. Had anyone allowed me to figure out things for myself when I was a baby?

In class a few days later, Rachel was lying on her back in the infant room, her two favorite toys—a shiny copper bowl and some beads—on the floor at her side. She looked at these objects with interest, reached toward them, and when she could not reach them, whimpered a little and looked toward me. I wanted to help her as I always had, but I remembered what Magda had said, "Wait." Many times Rachel reached for an object and became increasingly frustrated when she could not retrieve it, and she started to cry. It was painful for me to watch how she would turn toward an object, reach tentatively toward it, whimper or cry, then return to her back. It was difficult to acknowledge that she had learned to give up so easily because of my unnecessary help. Although she had the motor ability to reach an object, she didn't have the will to get it by herself. I had taught her helplessness.

Gradually, through months of patient observation, guided by Magda, I was able to quiet myself enough to sit back and allow Rachel the opportunity to struggle. I began to respect her for her courage, patience and persistence; and she found joy in her own self-directed activity.

Magda offered me an opportunity as an adult to relearn what I hadn't learned well as a child. As I learned to trust my daughter, I learned to trust myself.

6. The Responsibility of Parenthood

SOME PARENTS WANT TO believe that having a baby should not change their lives. But becoming a parent is one of the greatest changes in an adult's life, for better or worse. Why deny it? Why ignore it?

Nobody said it was easy to be a parent. Parenting takes time. It is like any job you train for. If only we could think of parenthood in these terms. Realistically, parents must know the consequences of their choices—having a child or not having a child, accepting a job or not accepting a job.

Before becoming a parent, consider two major difficulties:

- **The "Ongoingness" of Being a Parent.** Even if the child is not at home, you never stop being a parent. It is a terrific psychological burden to know and think and feel that, "This is my child and I am responsible for his well-being." It's a sense of "un-freeness."

- **The Technicality of Being a Parent.** This is the nitty-gritty—the basics, if you will. You simply must do certain things, go through definite caregiving motions while parenting. Whether you want to stay in bed or not, the child still demands ongoing care.

You must mentally plan for this parenting job as well as physically plan for it. You must make room for this child/job in your lives. If you decide that, yes, you choose to have a child, then you must accept the responsibility that goes with that choice. You must accept the involvement (time, space, emotion, availability) and a certain giving up or delaying of egotistical needs. Parents must realize this—there is no other way.

The Conflict of Needs

The conflict for parents is that they would like to do everything, not give up anything. Every parent makes his own choices.

Parents are torn between contradictory advice.

Some advise, "You, the parent, have the right to live your own life and the baby has to adjust to it." This usually means that parents take the infants wherever they go, driving them from place to place, expecting them to behave—shopping, visiting, in movie theaters, on a ski tour or wherever. The infants cannot behave according to their own needs. When they cry, they are hushed. They have to adapt to the needs of their parents. Their biological timetables are disrupted, and they become appendages to their parents' lives.

According to other advice, parents should give up everything just to serve the baby. But this is neither healthful nor realistic. To be always needed, always available, can drain any parent's energies. Seldom are guidelines given for mutual adaptation.

The RIE guidelines can help you to be sensitive to both your baby's and your own needs.

Parents must really take a good, introspective look at themselves and seriously question: "What kind of person am I?" "Where am I really going? What is my real goal?" It would be a good idea to question seriously what a child really needs before they have that child.

RIE emphasizes the benefits of infants' spending peaceful, uninterrupted time following their biological rhythms of falling asleep when sleepy and eating when hungry, rather than their having to adjust too soon to external schedules and unrealistic expectations. First, we have to let the child develop his own rhythm; and then later he can adjust more into adult life.

Think of having a baby as a unique time that you can both enjoy—it never comes back again. And that is the time for you to invest, to put in time. This is a time of letting go, a time to feel at ease, not hurried, not pushed, not wanting to achieve. If you are wanting to do something else while you are with your children, this ambivalence, this being torn, can make this time more difficult. (That does not mean you cannot also make arrangements and go away at times.) You still have the rest of your life to do all the things that you want to do.

An Investment in the Future

Parents need to know also that there is a certain amount of investment: "I will do this now and later reap the benefits."

In our society, very few things are done with the thought, "How will what I do now affect my child one year, ten years, twenty-five years from now?"

If parents would think about and plan for parenthood, there would be more happy children and parents. It is so important for a young child to start with good experiences in his own family. For two or two and a half years, maybe the parents could let go of other activities. Because this kind of timely investment is what ultimately may help produce secure, independent, self-sufficient children.

The more you invest in those first early years of parenting, the easier your life could be later on. You won't have to be a slave to a child who has been raised with aware, respectful attention. It can be the difference between nagging, neglected (withdrawn or aggressive) children and those who will make it in life independently, with strength and self-confidence.

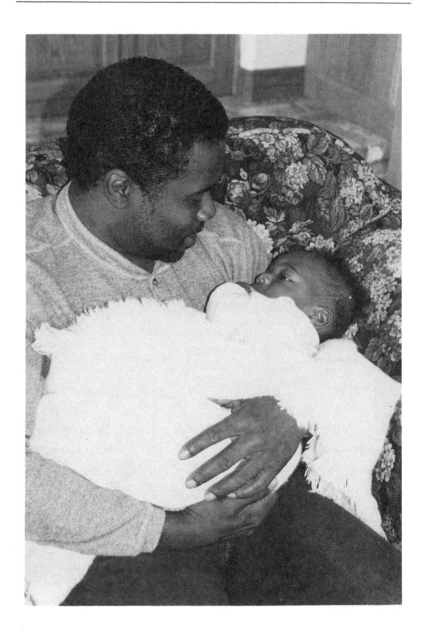

7. At Home with a Newborn

THE FIRST DAYS, WEEKS and months are a time of turmoil. Feelings of relief, joy mixed with doubts, anxieties, insecurities, despair, tiredness, tiredness, tiredness. Exhaustion makes any parent wonder, "Am I doing the right thing? Why is my baby so upset? Why can I not soothe her, what am I doing wrong?"

I would love to reassure new parents, particularly mothers, and tell them this is the way almost all new parents feel. Never before has your life changed so drastically. The beloved invader has disrupted your priorities, your schedule, your rhythm; you can no longer eat when hungry or sleep when exhausted.

One reason having a newborn is so difficult is because it feels *so important*. All new parents bring their own experiences, role models, and expectations of themselves to this new role. Wanting to "make it perfect" makes parents vulnerable; and if things do not go ideally, they may get angry with themselves and the baby. Anger is often followed by guilt and helplessness.

It is a stressful time. Parents cope in different ways. Some mothers deny the importance of the situation; they pretend that nothing has changed and that they are ready to throw a party three days after giving birth. Other mothers cannot accept that giving birth is the first separation; they need to hold on to their babies physically. Still other parents have difficulty making space in their lives for the baby. And yet others believe that, if they do not rush to a crying baby, the baby will be harmed.

What I would like to say is this: you are getting acquainted with a human being who will be among the most important people for you throughout your whole life. Give it time. The more open you are, the more interested in the uniqueness of this new being, the easier the process of mutual adaptation will become.

View this period with a newborn as learning to know each other and as an opportunity to learn about yourselves as never before. You might even "program" yourselves by saying over and over, "You, my baby, are so lucky to have us as parents, and we are so lucky to have you as our child."

Taking Care of Yourself

What does it take to start out well? To know, accept and like yourself. This will help you to know and accept your own vulnerability. For example, if you know that you become irritable when you get hungry, feed yourself.

The most difficult part of having a new baby is not having enough rest. You can give yourself much more time to rest if you do not expect yourself to do anything else than take good care of yourself and the baby.

When you have a newborn, especially your first, *do get help.* Your own mother or mother-in-law is seldom the right person. (She may be, if you feel really comfortable around her and she is not critical. Do these angels exist?) A good friend or a trusted hired person may work out the best. In some societies every new mother is naturally provided such help. Your helper should do all household chores, pamper you, but care for the baby only when you are too tired. Let go of duties and give yourself free-floating, timeless times like a young baby. Rest as much as possible. Have someone available so that you can have free time for yourself!

Living with an infant means living in a different time zone

and often in a strange emotional climate. Never before did you have to cope with so little sleep, constant tiredness, the burden of always being on duty, and an array of nagging doubts about your competence as a parent. You cannot rehearse for those first months. So much is new—the baby, the situation, the reaction of the other parent, and, most of all, your own feelings.

Some mothers and fathers feel scared when they notice how time stands still yet also flies by, how the outside world fades away and is replaced by baby's smiles and cries.

Dear new parent, do not be scared. Give in to the rhythm of a new biological clock; you will not stay in this place of time distortion forever. You will get back in the demanding, pushy, hustle-bustle of "normal" life in due time. Think of this as a kind of vacation on an island with no clocks, no duties other than responding to your own and your baby's rhythm and needs.

Mothers and fathers, be open to the new experience. Allow yourselves to emerge as new parents, and allow your baby to emerge as a new person. Try not to want to shape him, but rather accept his personal characteristics, his tempo and style.

Taking Care of Your Baby

The agenda for newborns and parents is to learn about each other and slowly develop a dialogue. It helps if you actually talk to your baby. (See, *Talking to Your Baby*, page 33)

What cues does a newborn baby give? Quite likely he cries, shows discomfort, or sleeps.

What parents expect of their babies and the way their babies realistically behave are often quite different. You may have expected a plump, smiling baby—instead, you look at your newborn and see a deformed head, blueish, wrinkled face and a skinny, hairy body. You may have expected to know what your baby needs—instead, your baby cries and cries, it alarms you and you do not know what she needs or what to do. (You might not feel *so* alien if you have visited newborn wards in hospitals and seen many newborns, or if you have watched parents with very young children and learned that all babies cry.)

No matter how simple an environment is, a baby may be overwhelmed by too much stimulation. Everything is new, and nothing functions easily yet. You can help your newborn adapt to all that newness by making the environment less loud, less bright, to allow your child to learn step by step, so he's not bombarded. Create a peaceful place; keep the newborn in a cozy place such as a bassinet; slowly and gently meet his needs for food, hygiene and holding.

It will take time, it must take time—lots of time—to learn to understand each other. Eventually, infants cry less and parents feel more and more secure.

A Peaceful Beginning

Regularity and predictability help babies develop their inner rhythms of sleeping, eating and alertness. It is best if babies can spend the first six to eight weeks undisturbed in their own environment at home and for parents to give themselves time without extra activities. If at all possible, I would try not to interrupt the baby's patterns by taking her with me to do errands.

Allow the infant to develop her biological rhythm first and then slowly ease the infant into to the life of the family. Eventually you and your baby will develop a peaceful, predictable rhythm of life.

The way you begin life with your newborn will set a pattern, a kind of blueprint for future relationships. And while it may seem too difficult to stay home for a while and postpone all those "self-fulfilling" activities in the world outside, believe me, it will be time well spent, learning about the daily wonder of a new human being, your own child.

And a Word for Grandparents

I want to remind grandparents that what everyone wants from an important relationship is attention, an open receptiveness. It may be that the best way to help your children offer this attentive relationship to their new baby is for you to offer just the same relationship to them.

As a grandparent, do not expect performance (to be a good mother or father) from the new parents. Accept them and this stage of their struggle. Cook and clean. Don't criticize.

As familiar with infants and parents as I was, I felt typically uncertain and unsure the first weeks with my own child. I almost felt, when his father would say, "Here's your mom," that he was referring not to me but to someone else.

After listening to Magda and studying RIE materials for years, I planned to give my full attention to nursing, diapering, bathing, etc. This takes commitment on my part, and I have found that it works well for me, although it surprises some people around me.

My expectations were often different from the reality of my life. While nursing Scott, I felt I had this open, available attitude and was fully present. I expected and was ready to gaze fully into my son's eyes and drink in and share the affectionate bond we were creating. The reality was that Scott was interested in nursing and his own world. Only occasionally did he invite me in and then only briefly. I kept waiting, and truthfully I wondered, "Why couldn't I read a book or talk on the phone? He would never notice." Here

I was creating this lovely time to be together and he was too busy to do it my way.

Luckily for me, because I believed in the RIE philosophy, I disciplined myself to continue my approach of allowing Scott to develop his own rhythm. Remarkably for me, he chose Mother's Day to look up and stare into my eyes long and full. Thanks to RIE and my commitment to be fully present in these times, I was able to notice the shift and to appreciate the change and the moment.

8. Talking to Your Baby

NOBODY KNOWS when exactly an infant begins to understand language. But infants do begin to pay attention to the world around them slowly and gradually from birth.

To talk to your baby from the first hour of her life is not only pleasant and soothing to the baby, it can be a relief for you, the parent, to say how you feel and what you want. It is also the beginning of a lifetime of communication.

Expressing Your Feelings and Thoughts

Just tell the baby how you feel and what you think; do not censor your feelings or thoughts.

"I wish I could make these first days and weeks easier for you and for me."

"I know you have to adapt to so many new things."

"Now I see how much more comfortable it was before you were born. You were growing and floating, with no effort, no struggle. Now you feel tired, hungry, your tummy aches. So much noise, so much light, so many changes."

"I want to help you, but so often I feel helpless."

"All these books make it even more difficult."

"I am so tired, I am scared, my life will never be the same again."

"I must be responsible, I don't want to be responsible. Mommy... I want my own mommy, I am still a child...."

"Oh, my sweet baby, you are so beautiful, those tiny hands,

fingers, and eensy weensy nails."

"I feel happier than ever. I want to learn to be your mother. Help me."

I chose these quotes from the many I have heard from mothers and fathers in our program. Most first talked to *me* but after repeated reminders did begin to talk to their own babies, and they felt better doing so.

The Prescription for Language Development

Rather than teach language purposefully to your baby, communicate, listen and read your baby's cues. Then simply talk to him as though he understands.

For a long time it may feel as if it is only one-sided, but delightful surprises in your baby's responsiveness will convince you he was putting together all your words, gestures and facial expressions all along.

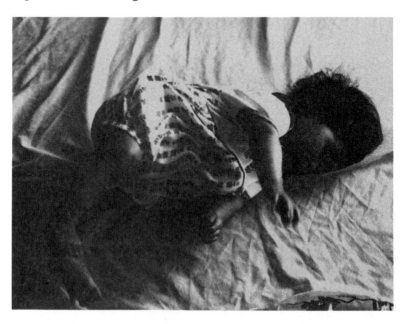

9. On Their Backs, Free to Move

YOUNG BABIES ARE MORE comfortable, more free to move, when placed on their backs rather than on their stomachs.

For many, many years, RIE's recommendation to place infants on their backs was the opposite of what most pediatricians, nurses and other experts believed and recommended. Thankfully, this has changed.

Newborn babies usually do not keep their heads up, and, for that reason, do not feel comfortable on their stomachs. And because they cannot hold their heads up, they cannot look around, and their visual field is limited to the patch of blanket in front of them.

On his stomach, a very young infant may try a few times to raise his head, then give up and stay more or less immobile. Or he may continue bobbing his head, accepting the strain and discomfort as a normal condition. What else can he do in that position?

Now let us look at the same baby on his back. With no strain, he can turn his head fully from one side to the other, looking around, learning about his immediate environment, and strengthening his neck muscles. His rib cage is free, so he can breathe more easily and deeply. He can easily stretch his arms and legs.

Observing Your Baby's Development

Having a very young baby seems to distort time. Every day feels like it never ends. When you are watching your baby continually, especially during the first months, it appears that nothing ever changes and that the baby does not do anything new or exciting.

Yet, with the aid of time-lapse photography, you could see how movements are changing from jerky to becoming smoother, how eyes are more focused, and of course how the baby suddenly looks like a "real person," a "social being" with the appearance of the first smile.

As you develop the art and skill of observing your baby, you will also see that every experience, day in and day out, is a learning experience for him.

Your baby senses differences of feelings—hunger or satiation, pain or comfort, sleepiness, drowsiness or wakefulness. Things (his hands, for instance) move in and out of his vision, his mouth finds a hand and sucks on it, a particular voice and face (yours) become more familiar and bring relief. All these are most meaningful and useful pieces of learning for a baby.

Babies may learn several things through one action. The sensation of finding his thumb can be called eye-hand-mouth coordination and can also be considered the forerunner of play. When your baby looks at an object, reaches for it and eventually grasps and moves it, he manipulates, he interacts with the world and makes things happen. Again, this is the beginning of play.

Most parents of very young babies live with constant anxiety about how well their babies are doing. Doctors seldom have time to observe how a baby moves naturally, on his own initiative; instead, they usually look at "milestones" to get a general idea of where a baby falls on the average curve of development. I wish they would remember and emphasize to parents that there is no one single point at which infants "should" reach these milestones.

How can a new parent gain confidence? My advice is... watch your baby. Respond to your baby. Enjoy what your baby is doing right now. As you observe and appreciate your baby's movements, his growing abilities, his exploration of his world, just think of all the pride and joy you can feel every day!

From Back to Stomach

One day, your baby will turn onto his side and later onto his stomach. He may be quite surprised by finding himself in that new position. He may struggle and possibly succeed in either freeing his arm (which usually gets caught under the body), or he may cry to let you know that he needs your help. In that case you could pick him up and place him back on his back and see how he behaves. If he is the adventurous type, he may wiggle and struggle to get to the new position. If he is more cautious, he may move slowly, looking around with some apprehension.

But no matter how he responds to the surprise of turning over the first few times, he will soon be able to turn onto his stomach at will, hold his head and chest up, and look around within a wide horizon. And that will be the perfect time for him to be, and to benefit from being, on his stomach.

When I saw my daughter trying to turn over by herself, I wanted to rush in. It was as if I saw myself writhing on the floor, incapacitated, like a beetle trying to flip itself over. I had trouble separating her struggle from my own. I took a deep breath and trusted Magda's ideas. I remained a supportive presence as she tried and tried. My daughter showed me that I could tolerate her

grappling with the inevitable change which needed to take place. She wanted to move on her own steam. She tried and tried and tried again. I tolerated her need to struggle, and I learned to be less afraid of my own struggles.

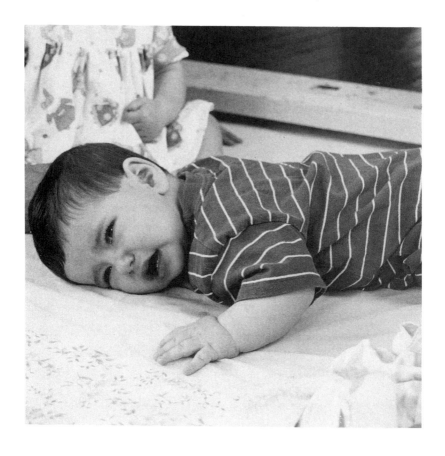

10. Crying and Colic

MANY BABIES CRY a lot during the first weeks, even the first three months.

There is no magic formula to know what your baby needs. It takes time, patience and continuous observations to learn first to differentiate among a baby's reasons for crying, and then to respond appropriately.

Nothing really prepares you to experience your own feelings of empathy, irritability, helplessness or maybe even rage when you hear your baby cry. However, it may help to remember that your baby comes into a world where everything is brand new.

Adapting to Changes

Babies have to learn to adapt to a very different life from the one to which they were accustomed in the womb. They need to sort out sensations coming from within and a barrage of stimuli coming from the outer world. They may feel lots of discomfort, and they express their discomfort by crying.

Their discomfort may be from hunger, pain, feeling too cold or too warm, sudden changes in position, or too much noise, light, or activity around the child. (An often-repeated belief is that babies cry when bored. Actually, they cry when *over*-stimulated.)

Sometimes a change from wakefulness to sleep, and vice-versa, are vulnerable transitional times. (See, *Sleeping*, page 91) Also, contrary to common belief, babies do not cry because they are wet. They do cry, however, when they have a diaper rash which is irritated by a wet diaper or when the wet diaper causes them to feel cold. A very young baby may cry to discharge energy.

It takes babies time to find out how they can help themselves. Eventually they learn how to get rid of gas bubbles, how to relax and fall asleep, how to suck most efficiently, etc.

Responding to a Crying Baby

Crying must be responded to. But *how* is a more complicated issue. To follow the advice, "Do not let your baby cry," is practically impossible. At times the harder a mother or father tries to stop the baby's crying, the more anxious everyone becomes.

What different parents do seems to be greatly influenced by their own needs and by their beliefs. The parent who likes to eat might feed the baby often; another parent who feels too cold or hot might cover or undress the baby. Other parents might pick up, jostle, carry around or rock their babies based on what they read or are told by "experts."

The way a parent responds to the baby also "conditions" the baby to expect specific responses (feeding, covering, rocking). Instead of responding to real need, the parent may respond to a created need, conditioned by the parent.

For example, an anxious and irritated parent (crying does irritate!) will most likely do what brings the fastest relief—give the breast or bottle. The baby almost always accepts it, calms down and often falls asleep. Of course, this *is* the right solution *if* the baby is hungry. However, if the baby has other needs (for instance, being tired or having pain), she will learn to expect food in response to these other needs, and grasp the breast or bottle even though she is not hungry. Fast, easy solutions work to relieve immediate tension but can result in forming bad habits. (See, *Thumb vs. Pacifier*, page 49, and *Feeding*, page 83)

40

Calm Dialogue

How *can* you help? Respond to your baby by letting him know that you are there and that you care.

First, do accept that you don't understand instinctively what exactly makes your baby cry, nor what to do about it. Next, rather than responding mechanically with one of the usual routines of holding, feeding or changing your baby, to stop the crying, try quietly talking to your baby.

Remember, crying is a baby's language—it is a way to express pain, anger, and sadness. Acknowledge the emotions your baby is expressing. Let him know he has communicated.

For example, you might tell him, "I see you're uncomfortable. And hearing you cry really upsets me. I want to find out what you need. Tell me. I will try to understand your cues and, in time, you will learn to give them to me." Or, "I see you are unhappy. I wish I knew what is making you unhappy." Then think out loud. "Could it be that your diaper is wet? I don't think you are hungry, because you just ate. Maybe I've been holding you long enough and maybe you want to be on your back for a while." This is the start of lifelong, honest communication.

It will take your baby some time to function more smoothly, to relax, to anticipate and respond to your care. Do not just try to stop the crying. Respect the child's right to express his feelings, or moods. (See, *Authentic Infant, Competent Child*, page 71). Try to find and eliminate discomfort.

Your baby will respond to your focused attention, your calm voice. Talking softly and gently, slowly bringing your face closer, gently picking him up, safely cradling him in your arms, then slowly putting him back in his crib, will eventually reassure and calm him.

Colic

Fairly often I meet families with very young infants who "have colic." From my observations, a frantic child brings about frantic parents doing incredibly frantic things to "calm" the baby. Taking them on walks, driving them in cars in the middle of the night, rocking and moving them side to side or up and down—my question is, why?

All healthy babies cry. We would worry if they didn't cry—no infant can be raised without crying. Respond to the baby, reflecting that you are there and that eventually you will learn to understand the reasons for the crying.

Do not start crazy tricks. Infants do not need them at any age, and neither do you. Do not make babies dependent on distractions that you do not want them to depend on later.

Your baby will learn to be calm from calm parents in a calm atmosphere.

An Alternative to Other Advice

In our classes, parents sometimes find that the RIE approach is the exact opposite of what they have been told by many, including pediatricians. However, RIE's calm approach has often been helpful because the colic seems to diminish when excess stimulation is removed from the baby's experiences.

With Ethan's colic, I followed every suggestion and piece of advice I received. I walked the floor with him; I picked him up and put him down, over and over again. I put him in a bouncer seat, I put him in front of a window, I took him for car rides, I put him in his car seat on top of the running dryer. I carried him around

in a sling. Still, Ethan screamed out, and I screamed in silence. After four months, I knew I had to make some changes.

When I visited my first RIE class, I was so impressed by the babies there. But these children were nothing like my child, I rationalized. Ethan could never play calmly and independently on *the floor while I sat nearby. Oh no, Ethan was a "high needs" baby. He needed* me. *However, desperation proved an effective motivator.*

I went home and put Ethan on the floor, on his back, and placed some appropriate items around him. I resisted, with great difficulty, the urge to shake a toy in his face or demonstrate how to manipulate it. Over the next few days an amazing thing began to happen. Ethan began to stretch his contracted and rigid limbs. He began to roll over and gain control of his wobbly neck. The most exciting development, however, was his growing self-awareness and self-confidence. His newfound freedom resulted in my own.

Four months of RIE classes have had a profound impact on us both. "Profound?" some people ask. Well, until you've survived the type of colic that causes your child to hold his breath, turn purple and break into a sweat before letting out a wake-the-dead scream every hour of every day, you don't have a clue how horrible it is. The last thing Ethan needed was more *stimulation. RIE provided us with a gentle, calm, relaxed alternative to the chaotic and frenetic "solutions" offered by well-meaning friends and relatives.*

11. Holding

YOUNG BABIES NEED both to be held and to be able to move freely in their cribs.

Often parents believe that holding is good, being left alone in a crib is not. I believe babies need both.

There are sound physiological reasons why a newborn should not be held all the time. To begin with, he must adapt to his new capabilities outside the womb, by kicking, stretching, curling and uncurling his body. In a crib, he can do this at will—and with ease. I see lots of infants hanging on their mothers or fathers in carriers. The babies are cramped and confined; any movement by the parent compresses them further into the carrier. Whenever the parent moves about or gesticulates, it is like a "mini-earthquake" for the baby!

Parents who carry their babies most of the time are not giving their infants the opportunity to move according to their readiness.

There are also psychological reasons why around-the-clock holding is not developmentally sound. Parents often say to me, "I want to hold my baby all the time to show him how much I love him." Most animals can show affection only through touch, but we humans have an extensive, varied and refined repertoire of ways to demonstrate love. To me, a mature, evolved person shows love by respecting the *otherness* of the beloved. You become a good parent not only by listening to your instinctive messages but by paying close attention to your baby, by observing the infant. Sensitive observation flows from respect. (See, *Learning to Observe ...*, page 63). How often I see parents holding their babies, or carrying them in contraptions close to the body, without paying the slightest attention to them. Isn't this somewhat like putting a pacifier in the mouth? It soothes or distracts the baby, who becomes "hooked" on an artificial solution to real problems.

Oh, yes, babies have problems. Hunger, discomfort and the need for sleep are all pressing urges. One of the first tasks a baby confronts is to learn to express these needs. Engaging her parent is nothing less than a triumph of communication.

Mutual understanding is a long, ongoing process. A baby's life is more than "I'm hungry—I cry—you feed me." What about "I'm tired—I cry"? A parent's task is to learn to read the baby's cues in order to meet these needs appropriately. Basic needs should be met. A parent who reads the infant's cues accurately and meets his needs is reinforcing the child's ability to give clear cues. But a parent who misinterprets may overfeed a tired baby who really needs to be allowed to sleep. Similarly, constant holding does nothing to help a baby recognize the difference between being alone and being with someone—I mean really *with* someone, eye-to-eye, genuinely engaged.

Before attending RIE classes, I had carried my daughter everywhere. Starting from three months, I soon learned that I could let go and still stay profoundly connected. My daughter taught herself to roll over and sit up and walk, teaching me in the process that I could let her. She taught me that there are all kinds of things she can do without me.

※

With Tia's crying, the only thing that seemed to help—but not always, and most of the time not completely—was holding her. I wondered what had happened to the peaceful baby I had expected to lie independently and happily on the floor. My limited understanding of RIE led me to feel I was failing the philosophy because I needed to hold her so much.

In my frantic phone call to Magda, I asked what to do with a baby that only wants to be held. Magda's answer stunned me: "Hold her," she said.

I almost dropped the phone. Was this the same woman who advocated respect for the infant's autonomy and independence? She continued, "Do you think RIE is that inflexible?"

Not only did I think there was one RIE way of parenting, I also thought there was only one kind of baby I could have: a cooing, smiling angel. The reality of my screaming infant had shattered that image, and I was left confused and disoriented. It dawned on me slowly that holding her a lot didn't mean we were rejecting the RIE ideals, it meant we were respecting a newborn's need and responding to our own needs as well. In those first few months we felt better about Tia's crying when we held her.

Now I can better understand Magda's answer: there is nothing non-RIE about holding a crying baby, but the parent needs to be aware of what they're doing and why they're doing it. Holding a baby nonstop for two hours may be disrespectful to yourself, not to mention your arms; and bouncing an unhappy baby is not necessarily being sensitive to the infant's real needs. By engaging in this behavior, we may in fact be creating a need that didn't exist before.

It would have been easier, perhaps, if we had known more

about the developmental stages of infancy. We weren't able to see the first trying period as a passing phase; for us it seemed Tia would never enjoy being put down on the floor. Gradually, though, the good days got more frequent and the bad days faded from memory. By the time Tia was three months old, she began to fulfill my image of the baby I thought I'd have—although the reality of my daughter was much richer and more varied than anything I had imagined.

12. Thumb vs. Pacifier

SOME INFANTS ARE BORN with their thumbs in their mouths or even have been known to suck in the womb. We know from literature as well as from observing infants that they have a strong need for sucking. It is often referred to as the sucking instinct or reflex.

Sucking also stops crying. As a result, many crying children are given the breast or the bottle, not because they need food, but to end their crying. Thrusting the breast, the bottle, a pacifier or a teether into a crying infant's mouth is one of the most often-used calming devices. It is fast, handy, and it works.

Sucking is an instinctual need, and adults have an instinctual rather than objective reaction to it. When a mother says, "It makes me sick to see my five-year-old put his thumb in his mouth," or "How disgusting this two-year-old looks sucking on his blanket," it is obvious that deeper emotional layers in the parent are touched.

Throughout history, thumb-sucking has aroused many strong feelings. It has been called a bad habit and has been blamed for producing protruding teeth and a disobedient, withdrawn or insatiable child. Society has been "up in arms" about oral gratification. Parents have been advised to restrain the baby physically by tying her arms, pulling sleeves over her hands, using mittens or elbow splints, or putting something bitter-tasting on the thumbs. Gentler interferences have included pulling out the thumb, giving a substitute, and distracting, bribing, or showing dislike.

Any of these reactions gives an infant the message—at a very early, impressionable age—that something that feels so good, comforting, natural, and easy is bad. This may lead a child to believe that after feeling good you will encounter something bad as a consequence; or that you have to pay the price for feeling good; or that you do not deserve to feel good. It is like planting seeds of doubt and insecurity about one's own goodness or the goodness of the outside world.

Thumb vs. Pacifier

The thumb belongs to the infant. She has to discover it and learn how to use it as part of her own body. It is always available. It doesn't fall on the floor and get dirty or get lost when needed. The infant can put it in her mouth and pull it out according to her own needs and desires. In the process, she learns how to soothe herself and how to become self-reliant. When there are no misgivings about it, she will use it when and for as long as she really needs it. Yet some parents frown on thumb-sucking.

I do not know when the pacifier was invented, but it is a very old device. Perhaps in an earlier era, keeping a baby quiet helped secure survival. In times when the common belief was that infants should be kept completely passive and helpless, infants were swaddled, rocked and prevented from having any activity—and, indeed, they became passive and quiet.

In our days, pacifiers are given mainly for the following reasons: to stop crying, to meet the need for sucking, to put an infant to sleep, to soothe colic, and to prevent thumb-sucking.

The pacifier is a plug. It does stop a child from crying, but the question is, does an infant have a right to cry? Should an infant be allowed to express her feelings and communicate them? Plugging her mouth gives the message, "Don't do what comes naturally. Do what pleases me, your parent. I am in control of how you should feel and how you should show your feelings."

When anything is put into a young infant's mouth, she starts sucking. However, is her real need for sucking met, or is the pacifier given when the parent interprets the infant's need for it? When the pacifier is used to put an infant to sleep, it is often when the adult decides that the infant should sleep. In addition, there is no proof that sucking the pacifier helps relieve colic better than sucking the thumb.

Many parents prefer the pacifier to thumb-sucking. Why this fierce debate? What are the real or imagined dangers of thumb-sucking? Parents complain about being awakened many times at night because the pacifier fell out of the baby's mouth. Yet they prefer this situation to one where the infant is in control. Some worry that the child will be sucking his or her thumb in kindergarten, or longer. Others claim they can always throw out the pacifier when the child becomes too old for it. Again, the parent is in control.

The issue is not a simple preference of pacifier vs. thumb. The real issue is, who is in control?

Julia went through an amazing process of learning to suck her thumb. During the first three weeks of life there were moments when we thought Julia would love to have something to suck on. One could see the furious sucking movements she was making. At around two and a half weeks of age, Julia ended up with her thumb in her mouth by accident. She delighted in being able to suck her thumb. The next few days she tried, without success, to

put her thumb in her mouth. Sometimes her efforts would lead to frustration and fussiness. We wondered whether we should intervene but decided to let her struggle. When she succeeded in putting her thumb in her mouth, the satisfaction she showed was rewarding for us to see. Sometimes Julia would simply put her thumb in her mouth for the sake of putting it in her mouth. Other times she would suck on it to soothe herself.

Her next struggle came when she wanted to learn how to put her other thumb in her mouth. Figuring out how to control her right thumb took several more days and a considerable amount of struggle. When frustrated, at least she could give herself solace by turning to her left and sucking on her left thumb. Once she gained control of her right thumb, she was happy. She would suck on her right thumb for a while, and then on her left one and so on. We believe none of this discovery could have happened when it did if Julia had been given a pacifier.

An unanticipated benefit to the thumb-sucking discovery was that it helped Julia take care of herself during the night. We discovered that she did not necessarily sleep through the night. Instead of being awakened in the middle of the night by crying, we were awakened by loud thumb-sucking! When she was not hungry, Julia had become able to soothe herself in the night through thumb-sucking. We quickly learned to sleep through the thumb-sucking. If Julia needed us, she would cry.

13. At Their Own Time, and In Their Own Way

INFANTS ALWAYS DO what they *can* do—and they should not be expected to do what they are not ready for. At RIE we allow infants to do what they are ready and willing to do.

Every infant develops according to his or her built-in, predetermined time schedule. There is a wide gap between the time some infants sit or stand up, make their first steps, or utter their first words. There are no later consequences whether an infant starts to walk or talk very early or very late. Why, then, don't we wait patiently until it happens naturally? In other words, at the perfect time.

Natural Gross Motor Development

Every baby moves with more ease and efficiency if allowed to do it at his own time and in his own way, without our trying to teach him. A child who has always been allowed to move freely develops not only an agile body but also good judgment about what he can and cannot do. Developing good body image, spatial relations, and a sense of balance helps the child learn not only how to move but also how to fall and how to recover. Children raised this way hardly ever have any serious accidents.

Learning by Moving

In many cultures people have been led to think that, unless infants are taught, they do not learn. Under the guise of teaching and caring have come tight swaddling, being tied to boards, being carried in slings and pouches, placed in infant seats, jumpers or walkers, being immobilized as well as exercised. (See, *On Teaching and Learning*, page 11) The fact that all "normal" children learn to walk clearly shows their amazing resilience.

There is evidence that gross motor development happens naturally when an infant has plenty of space to move in a safe, age-appropriate and challenging environment. However, some people find this hard to believe.

But if you watch babies who are allowed to move freely and without interference, you will see that they learn to move gracefully and securely and that, through endless repetition and practice, they become well balanced. When not interrupted, babies are totally absorbed in what they are doing. These kinds of sensory experiences *are* learning and are also a great pleasure for a parent to watch! A father who asked me whether he should exercise his baby or take him to a gym class was intrigued when I suggested that he imitate all his baby's movements for about one hour and decide then if his baby needed an additional workout.

Learning to see how infants move also means seeing how adults knowingly and unknowingly influence their movement. This is a key to understanding the basic RIE point of view.

The Concept of Readiness

In contrast to our approach, too often I have seen children taught, encouraged and expected to do what they are basically not ready to do. Too many infants are propped up when they cannot maintain a well-balanced sitting position, or are given a toy which they have neither freely chosen nor can freely manipulate. Similarly, putting infants into devices such as infant seats, walkers, swings, or bouncers restricts them from moving freely.

Such devices introduce positions or movements for which the infant is not yet ready. (See, *Equipment: What is Really Necessary?*, page 159)

If infants are ready to do something, they will do it. In fact, when they are ready, they *have* to do it.

When I visit centers or families, I often feel sad or frustrated because the children, to my mind, *are* doing beautiful things; the adults say, however, "But why don't they do something?"—and "something" is always something the children cannot do. When we give a child the message, "If only you would..." or "If only you wouldn't...," that child does not feel okay.

Try to feel you are that infant: you feel you have to perform, you have to do, you have to create something. If you are lying peacefully on your back, then you should be sitting up. Even if you cannot sit up, you should. You feel that the important people in your life expect something of you that you cannot deliver.

However, a child who cannot sit, cannot sit. Yes, you can prop pillows around an infant, but that only gives the illusion that he can sit. Sitting means that the infant has developed through all the stages from lying to sitting. Learning to sit is different from sitting. It does not happen the way many people think it does—by first putting a baby into a sitting position so he will learn.

Development Milestones

Research at Loczy[1] showed wide variation in development

---

[1] Loczy (now the Pikler Institute) is an internationally recognized center of observationally based research on infants. Much of the RIE philosophy is based on work done at Loczy. (See, *Reflections on My Work with Dr. Pikler*, page 185)

among normal Hungarian babies who had been allowed to reach milestones of motor development naturally. For example, it was quite normal for a baby to begin to turn from his back over to his stomach anywhere from 19 weeks to 39 weeks of age. A baby who could roll onto his stomach by himself began to play in this position (requiring holding the head up comfortably and being able to turn from back to stomach to back again) anywhere from 22 weeks to 41 weeks after birth. The average age range at which babies began to get themselves into a sitting position was 38 weeks to 16 months, and they began to play comfortably in a sitting position somewhere between 40 weeks and 16 months. So you see, the normal range was dramatically wide.

How can we tell whether our expectations are developmentally appropriate? By observing, accepting and enjoying what the infant is self-initiating and practicing all by himself.

While there are norms of average development, we should not be too concerned about them unless an infant is showing many signs of being "different" from other children of a similar age. Parents and professionals who wait for the next and the next "achievement" sadly miss the miraculous little changes which are occurring all the time.

14. Predictability: Helping Your Child Feel Secure

WHAT A VERY YOUNG infant needs is to be secure.

Security is almost a "body feeling" that an infant can sense. The way we pick up and carry an infant can support or decrease this feeling. (Have you seen babies being carried and their heads were wobbling? That does not give a feeling of security.)

Everything you do or do not do influences how an infant feels. We believe that if you do everything very, very slowly, and if you include the child, then the child feels he is a very important person. From birth on, we should try to include them.

When babies are bombarded with new stimuli, new places, new experiences, it is very difficult for them to adapt and to learn to trust.

In a predictable environment, and with regular, dependable schedules, they feel comfortable, cry less, and life is easier for both infant and parents. Infants who do not need to adjust to too much unnecessary stimulation will eventually regulate their sleeping and eating patterns. This regularity will, in turn, give parents some predictable time for their own needs and interests.

Dealing with Changes

Everything in life changes. Night to day, spring to summer, caterpillar to butterfly, infant to child to adult. Of all the stages

57

of human life, infancy is the time of the most rapid growth. This growth in all areas—physical, mental and emotional—means constant change. These are natural changes. There are also circumstantially imposed changes: wars, death, earthquakes, things over which we have little, if any, control. In everyday life we also have humanly imposed changes—some necessary, some unnecessary.

Infants' reactions to life and to the environment are, to a great extent, determined by the child's stage of development and change very quickly. Using time-lapse photography, we might see a five-month-old baby lying on the floor looking up at the table; at eleven months, she might be pulling herself up to the table; and at eighteen months, she might even have climbed to the top of the table. Same room, same table—only the baby would have changed.

Because babies grow and change so rapidly, we need to provide them with as much security as we can, to give them a firm base from which to cope with the changes that come both from the environment and from within themselves.

Infancy is the time to build this solid foundation. The more secure your child is, the more easily she can adapt to novelty. And your child will become secure if her life in general is peaceful and predictable.

A Predictable Daily Routine

"Predictable" means that, from the very beginning of her life, you tell your baby ahead of time when a change will happen—even a tiny change, such as "I will turn the light on," or "I will pick you up," or "I'll go to the bathroom now." Although her immediate reaction may be to ignore or protest the change, soon she will become confident in the face of changes.

It may seem contrary to prepare a child for our hectic world by providing a comfortable, predictable, constant daily routine. In fact, some parents wonder whether exposing a child to many changes early in life might not prepare her better for our fast-changing society. My answer is no. Being exposed to circumstances we cannot anticipate nor understand, and in which we cannot actively participate, makes us feel helpless, like riding on a perpetual merry-go-round. Anticipating a change, on the other hand, gives us a feeling of being prepared, of being in control. Also, the more secure we feel, the more flexible we become—like a good skier whose flexibly bent knees act as a shock absorber, protecting him from bumps.

Should we try to protect children from all change? No—this is impossible. We must each find a balance in our own lives. Dealing with the unexpected can be made easier by keeping a consistent, overall pattern. People move, get divorced, get married, have a new baby, or get a new job requiring a different time schedule. It is easier to cope with major changes if the small routines of life (such as bathing, dressing and going to bed) remain intact. You may occasionally bathe in a different tub, sleep in a different bed, but you still bathe, then sleep. From these simple routines self-confidence, security and consistency in the midst of change can be derived.

Traveling, Family Visits and Other Special Events

Parents often ask how to prepare infants for a vacation or family visit, a long drive, or any special event.

Plan to take with you many familiar objects—sheets, bed clothes, "blankies," toys, even a port-a-crib if possible, to recreate the child's own environment. Keep as many things similar as possible—daily schedules, foods, your own style of interaction with your child, etc. Through these simple routines, a child develops a sense of constancy, security, and self-confidence even in the midst of change.

What many parents find truly difficult is to "protect" the child from the "assault" of well-meaning family members and friends. My advice is to start out saying that you have learned that your child functions better when given time to adapt to new situations and people. Do not criticize what others do, just gently yet firmly stick to your own principles—for example, not letting your child be handed around like a ball.

Family and friends may tell you or think that you are crazy or exaggeratedly overprotective. Take the blame; quietly accept responsibility for your stance. Soon they will accept your "stubbornness" and may learn to enjoy you and your baby on your terms.

But no matter how well you handle the situation, you still may have difficulties after returning from a visit or a vacation. Try to re-establish the same routines you had before leaving home. You can say, "I know that at Grandma's house you stayed up later, but now we are back home again." If you are patient, understanding and consistent, things will go back to normal again fairly soon.

Interruptions

It distresses me to see the many unnecessary changes to which infants are subjected. Most adults do not even seem to be aware that they interrupt an infant, and they have difficulty understanding me when I try to explain it.

I like to make this analogy. If someone were to walk in on a scientist on the verge of discovering the secrets of the universe, would it occur to that person to interrupt with an inconsequential comment about the weather, or the new shoes she just bought? No, the scientist is doing very important research; and if interruption were necessary, an appropriate opening would be found.

But a baby? That same person might think nothing of picking up a baby—to see if a diaper should be changed, for example, or perhaps for no reason other than to pick up the baby. This baby may have been involved in very important research into how her hand disappears from view when she moves her arm this way and miraculously reappears when her arm goes the other way. With babies, as well as adults, one should consider whether an interruption is necessary; and if so, one should wait until an appropriate opening can be found. In this way, we demonstrate our respect for the importance of what infants are doing and learning at all times. (See, ... *and WAIT!*, page 67)

A Secure Environment

In summary, if our goal is for infants to be able to participate with us in their lives and care, they must be able to anticipate changes. A stable, predictable, secure environment is the best foundation an infant can have for developing the confidence and self-esteem necessary to handle changes in life.

From the very start, each time I placed Nathan in his car seat, I warned him before I closed the car door. "Here comes the door!" I'd say, and then WHUMP, the door would shut. After repeating this little ritual no more than ten times, I noticed that Nathan, only a few weeks old, would close his eyes before the door slammed. He was able to prepare himself, at his own level, for the loud noise and jarring motion.

🙣

As a result of Magda's teachings, I developed the habit of telling my daughter when I was going somewhere, if only into the next room, and also indicating how long I would be gone. I experienced a reflection of this interaction recently when we were playing on the beach. My daughter, at twenty months, decided to venture about fifteen feet to the swing set from the jungle gym where I was sitting. Looking back at me, she said, "Back," and held up her index finger to indicate one minute.

15. Learning to Observe ...

Babies COMMUNICATE from birth. If your attitude is, "I cannot know automatically what you need; please tell me," then the baby will learn to give you cues, and a dialogue will develop. If, on the other hand, parents superimpose their interpretations of the baby's problem, the infant may *un*learn to expect appropriate responses to her needs and learn to accept what the parents offer.

This is the difference between being understood and misunderstood. Being understood creates security, trust and confidence. Being misunderstood creates doubt both in oneself and in one's own perceptions.

So how can we try to understand rather than misunderstand? What should we do? The answer is, observe more, do less.

Observe More, Do Less

Is this an easy process? No way! In our society, we're trained to do, do, do. And if you don't, you *pretend* to do, do, do. You must act as if you are very busy, because being busy is virtuous. Not doing anything is considered laziness, and that's not highly appreciated. Nobody talks about being observant.

The more we do, the busier we are, the less we really pay attention.

To spend some time sitting peacefully in the room while your infant is doing her own thing, without wanting to play with her, teach her, or care for her—just being available to her—will make you much more sensitive to your child's needs, her tempo and her style.

This may sound easy, but in reality it is very difficult. You must develop the skills, the patience, the appropriate attitude.

Very few have learned the art of observing; most people do not appreciate the concentrated work involved. It means seeing not only what the baby does but also figuring out what she is learning in the process and whether or how adults should help.

Seeing "New"

Why is observation so difficult? Because we have the tendency to see what we "know," what we believe in, rather than what is happening in front of our eyes. Theoretically you would need to empty yourself of what you hope for your child and what you are anxious about—in other words, what you would like to see and what you are afraid to see. For a certain time you need to "detach" yourself and look as if you would see, for the first time, this little stranger whose needs you more often guess than know.

We must learn to see as a baby sees—new.

Let go of all the other issues that wander through your mind and really pay attention. Focus fully on everything your child does, trying to understand her "point of view." Try to observe what interests her, how she handles frustration, solves little problems (See, *Quality Time*, page 75). Infants do not yet speak our language but they give us many, many signs.

And what are the benefits?

If you learn how to observe and understand the personality of your child, the quality of your interactions will also improve.

Once you learn how to observe, how to pay full attention,

your relationship with other people, grown-ups included, will also change. You give them a gift by telling them with your attentive behavior, "You are worthy of my interest and full attention."

Every human being likes to be listened to, to get genuine attention, to feel understood, accepted, approved of and appreciated.

I think one of the hardest things we do each day when we come to work with the babies [at a RIE-accredited infant/toddler center] *is to let go of all the baggage we carry around with us. I have heard Magda say many times that we need to pretend that there is a* big *bowl sitting at the doorway, ready to be filled with preconceived ideas, bad moods, impatient feelings, stress, and even excess happiness. Let it go and enter the room peacefully, she says, ready to participate fully with each child. Why? Because anytime we are dealing with a baby who cannot talk about her needs, frustrations, and desires, and who relies on signals, eye contact, sounds, and gestures, we run the risk of projecting our own feelings, fears, disappointments, and emotions onto the baby—which would be a major miscommunication and loss of the baby's trust in getting her needs met. For instance, a caregiver with issues centering around food needs to be careful not to respond to a baby's hunger by overfeeding or underfeeding or forcing food. Or a caregiver who hasn't slept well may react to a baby's fussiness by assuming she needs a nap. Sometimes a caregiver will be laughing and overly exuberant with a baby, not seeing the uncomfortable look on the baby's face. Caregivers who have trouble with conflicts or communication may have a hard time allowing two babies to work out their differences their own way, always stepping in to stop them.*

There are many variations of this human phenomenon, and the only way one can guard against it is by making a conscientious effort each day to identify what the baggage is and then to leave it at the door. The more we enter into the day with an open mind and observe the babies, listen to them, get to know their ways of communication and allow them their individuality, the more we learn about the babies and *about ourselves.*

16. ... and WAIT!

ONCE, MANY YEARS AGO, I saw an infant lying on the floor who was trying to catch something in a very dreamy, beautiful way. I didn't see anything, but I knew that the child saw something. Only as I walked around did I realize that the dust in the air was creating a rainbow, and that's what the child saw.

That experience stayed with me as a symbolic reminder, so that now when people do things, I want to say, "That child may just see the rainbow—don't interrupt. Wait."

Time for Uninterrupted Play

The less we interrupt, the more easily infants develop a long attention span. According to many books, a baby has a short attention span; but that is not quite true. If infants are well cared for, if they can do what they happen to be interested in at that time, and if nobody interrupts, they have much longer attention spans than we give them credit for.

Contrary to grown-ups' expectations, infants usually do not get overly frustrated by struggles during play. When a toy gets caught or a ball rolls away, they may even enjoy the situation and certainly learn from it—if adults do not solve the problem for them.

To a degree, the child's response to potential frustrations is influenced by the adult's reaction. Even a very young child will look around to check out the adult's reaction when one of these puzzling, unexpected events occurs. A calm, observant comment, such as "Oh, the ball rolled away," will allow your baby to retain his role as initiator in his play and to choose how to handle the situation.

Sometimes parents who haven't been paying much attention will suddenly realize it and say something like, "Oh, you built such a nice tower!" And you know what happens? The child stops building the tower. Such an abrupt comment, rather than making a connection, interrupts play. If real sensitivity exists, then when the child looks up and seeks the parent's eyes, then the parent's eyes are quietly there. That can be the time to make a comment.

Selective Intervention

Wait! In so many situations, to wait means to allow problems to resolve themselves.

Selective intervention means knowing when *not* to intervene, and this is more difficult than intervening indiscriminately.

If an infant gets into a difficult situation (climbing up, for example), it is important to allow her to do whatever she can do, which means we must wait and wait and wait.

But we do come near so the infant knows we are available, which brings about a certain amount of security. Rather than give the message, "When you are in trouble, you scream and I rescue you," we would like to convey the feeling, "I think you can handle it, but if not, I am here."

Often you will find out that, even though you thought you had to help, the child didn't really need your help.

I prefer to wait until the infant really lets me know, "I cannot handle it any more." (And if this happens, it's very important to know why—is she tired?)

You might just ask, even a child who does not yet speak, "Do you need some help?" or, as a last resort, perhaps, "Do you want me to help you down?"

In providing infants with the minimal help they need to overcome an impasse, we demonstrate our trust in their competence and allow them to enjoy mastery of their own actions.

Nathan's first climbing experiments were with a set of low wooden boxes in his room. These crates are turned on their sides and serve as floor-level storage for his toys. At about eight months, Nathan began attempting to scale these crates. He would pull himself to standing, lean his body over the waist-high crate and try to squirm up. One afternoon, after about a week of trying, he figured out the mechanics necessary to achieve a kneeling position on top of the crate. Although I was a little nervous seeing him up there, he was so pleased with himself that I swallowed my anxiety and moved close to him without interfering.

After a few moments, Nathan decided it was time to get down—but how? He looked at the floor, and at me, and began to whine. I stayed close and responded to his complaints with quiet, encouraging remarks and made no offer of physical help. For three long minutes Nathan tried various methods of descent, rejecting each in turn, frequently looking at me and whimpering. When I did not "rescue" him, he would return to his work. Finally he got his legs over the edge, feet on the ground, and was off into the other room. He had solved the problem.

Thirty minutes later, he crawled back into the room and to the crate, climbed up to the top, paused an instant, then climbed down and crawled away, without looking at me once. It was as if he wanted to be sure he had mastered that skill.

17. Authentic Infant, Competent Child

An AUTHENTIC PERSON IS one who doesn't have to play a role all the time—someone who is true to himself or herself. If you want an infant to be authentic, you have to be interested in who that little person really is. That means that the less you assume about that baby, the more you will learn.

Adults often have a preconceived mold they try to squeeze an infant into—something *they* want the child to be. When that happens, the child may grow up not having a sense of who she really is or what she really wants because she lacks a core of authenticity.

Confusing Messages

Many years ago I wrote about the unforgettable, unpleasant experience we had when Dr. Emmi Pikler and I visited a swim class for young infants. I reported on the sensible speech the instructor made before the class, reassuring the parents that the goal was not to teach swimming but simply to help the children learn to enjoy the water. Right after this speech, however, she changed into a commanding sergeant and yelled, "Hold your children, immerse them 'til the neck! 'Til the nose! Over their heads! Have fun!" And indeed, the parents followed all instructions, including "Have fun," bursting into broad smiles, repeating, "Isn't this fun?" "We have fun," while looking into their babies' surprised and frightened faces. Only one mother, of an

71

apparently exhausted baby, said, "I think that is enough for you," and picked the baby up and rested her on the side of the pool.

How could these loving, caring parents not see or read their children's feelings? It looks like, "I see what I want to see," or "I enjoy it, you should enjoy it, too," or "You have no reason to be upset while I try so hard to do what I know is good for you."

What did these babies really learn or experience? From the child's point of view, how confusing it must be to feel miserable and see the most trusted person not noticing your anxiety but smiling at you. No wonder so many adults seek therapy, trying to sort out how they really feel.

I see similar insensitivities again and again. I have heard mothers say, "I love you so," at times when it was more likely that their true feelings were, "I cannot stand your crying anymore." Are these parents aware that they are brainwashing themselves and their children?

Infants as Objects?

This "double think" seems to begin very early, as parents approach their infants more as objects than as humans.

Some parents throw infants up in the air "because the baby loves it." Indeed, after many throws, infants have a similar anxiety-ridden smile (and tension-filled body) as children and adults have on roller coasters. Parents see what they want to see rather than the reality.

"You're okay," is repeatedly told to a child who hurts himself and does *not* feel okay. I would much rather give the child permission to feel the way she feels and then wait it out. Again the magic "waiting" works, because emotions have their beginning and their end—even tantrums have a beginning and an end.

Tickling is physically exciting and is often used by adults in order to change a sad or tired child into a giggly one. Sadness, discomfort, frustration—they are all valid human emotions. Why would we want to suppress them?

Whenever I hear or read statements which encourage grown-ups to initiate certain activities which "stimulate" the infants to respond (kissing the tummy, walking fingers, and "I'm gonna-get-you" are other examples), I feel uneasy. I consider tickling a young baby disrespectful. I prefer to be responsive to an infant's initiations rather than stimulating and exciting the infant.

I may be overly sensitive, but it even bothers me when I see an adult smiling at a crying, upset or sad child. Why do we want to manipulate young children's moods and feelings?

Maybe all this objectification is meant to prepare children to play the pretense games our society plays. Advertisements and commercials are based on people's gullibility to suggestions. The success of our whole economy depends on people's suggestibility—making intelligent people believe in the unbelievable but desired result a product promises (pounds and wrinkles disappear, etc.), confusing wishful thinking with reality.

I sometimes wonder whether we could function in a society where we could be more honest with each other. Must we hide our real feelings?

Genuine and Honest Communication

We should not stop babies from crying by automatically putting something in their mouths. Just as when an adult says, "You're okay," to a crying child, the adult who automatically puts something in the baby's mouth is not acknowledging what the child is communicating. Babies have a right to cry and feel what they feel with the knowledge that a kindly adult is there to help if possible.

Accept the feelings of your baby, positive as well as negative. And allow your child to learn about you.

Be genuine and honest in your interactions. You do not need to put on a sweet smile when you are awakened in the middle of the night. You are sleepy, so act sleepy.

Sensitive Observation

At RIE we encourage parents to learn to quiet down, to sit peacefully, to observe and to allow babies to be real.

There is one thing all of us value and desire. It is real attention, not fake; authenticity, not pretense. Maybe if we could train ourselves to pay attention, full undivided attention for just a short time every day (one, two or more times), we could learn about the other person. We would have to pay attention to facial expression, tone of voice, body language, posture, tension or relaxation, etc. And as we get sensitized and skilled in the art of observing, we may try the greatest challenge: to look inside—to see, observe and learn about ourselves.

Learning to observe your baby is a long and slow process. If your goal is to allow your baby to become a genuine, authentic being, it is the most worthwhile investment.

18. Quality Time

QUALITY TIME! WE ALL talk about it. We all want it, both for our children and for ourselves. But do we really know what quality time is all about?

It is full, unhurried attention. Under the right circumstances it is a peaceful, rewarding time for *both* parties because, ideally, it is a time of no ambivalence—one for open listening, trying to understand fully the other's point of view. This unique time can happen under many circumstances, which I divide into two themes.

"Wants Nothing" Quality Time – That's when the parent doesn't want to do anything with the infant, has no plans other than wanting simply to be with the child: just floor-sitting, being available, being there with all the senses awakened to the child; watching, listening, thinking only of that child. It sounds easy, but few can truly do it.

Most of us are used to, and conditioned to, *doing* something. *"Wants nothing"* time is different, more a time for taking in and waiting. We fully accept the infant's beingness just by our own receptive beingness. Our presence is telling the child that we are really there and aware. If you really feel that you should do something during this time, or if your mind is on what to cook, whom to call, etc., then it is not the right time.

This is a free-flowing space in which the child should not feel he has to perform, because the parent is not sending out the kind of demanding messages that say, "I am here now, what shall we do?" If the infant seems to ignore you and is doing something completely on his own, don't leave. It is very comforting for him to know you are there, really *there*, without any pressure to have to do something to keep your attention.

This separate play in the parent's presence teaches the child to depend on his own inner security. If you do this with a newborn, if you learn to see the child fully, you discover a person unfolding as you observe. *"Wants nothing"* time doesn't produce immediate results. Please remember this. *Everything*, especially something new, needs time and patience. You must plant and then reap; you put in what you feel is right, and then slowly it germinates. Quality time is an investment in the future of your child, as well as in the present. You are available, waiting; the child is the initiator.

"Wants Something" Quality Time – This is when you *do* have a goal of accomplishing something together, such as dressing, bathing, feeding, etc. This, too, should be regarded as quality time. You can make sure the child knows that this time is different from your *"Wants nothing"* time by saying, "Now I want to diaper you," "Now it's time to get dressed," etc.

This is a time when you work for cooperation, using the time for learning to do a task together when you expect the child to participate. It should become something you both enjoy doing together. Your *availability* is still there, except that during this time you also have *expectations*. This is the beginning of introducing and reinforcing discipline.

Around age two, a child's most important task is to become autonomous. Before this time, you and the child have what is called a "symbiotic" relationship: parent and child are almost like one. You depend emotionally on each other—and from this attachment, both eventually have to separate from each other.

This is the separation-individuation stage, when the child becomes an individual. This takes a long time. During this separation phase the child will try his wings by teasing, challenging and game playing.

There are two attitudes that are helpful in dealing with these games: 1) you enjoy and acknowledge this playfulness; but when it is time to go on, 2) you are *firm*. You allow a little time to play the game and let the child know you are playing; then you become firm and say that *now* it is time. You don't back off; you don't reverse your message: "We really have to get dressed. We've played, but now it's time. Can you do it yourself, or shall I do it?" Now we are not playing games with the infant because we want to get the job done. Try not to get angry. Be matter-of-fact and not aggressive. Anger only excites the child to want to play more. You don't respond to silly business at this stage. The play is over. "I would have liked to do it together, but now I have to do it for you. Maybe you can still help. Here, pull this up." Fooling around is very much part of development; but the children do have to cooperate later: *I'll dance with you and then you must dance with me.*

Growing Together

Quality time is a time of growth, movement, ebb and flow. If you can give these two kinds of quality time (*"Wants nothing"* and *"Wants something"* themes), then you are really growing with your children. It is the consistency of the time you are giving that does so much. Do not worry if you cannot get together every day; the rhythm of your togetherness will not be broken. It is what happens consistently, not mechanically, that counts. You can be together hour after hour in great *quantities* but not actually connect, see, hear or respond to each other. That is not what quality time is all about.

The beauty of this special kind of availability is the way it affects the older child and later the adult who was raised with it. You will find that they do not feel they have to be forced to talk. They can peacefully sit with the parent and then open up when they want to. The child does not feel manipulated.

What you do with your child is an investment for the future. Quality time is what everybody really wants: a gift of time and attention.

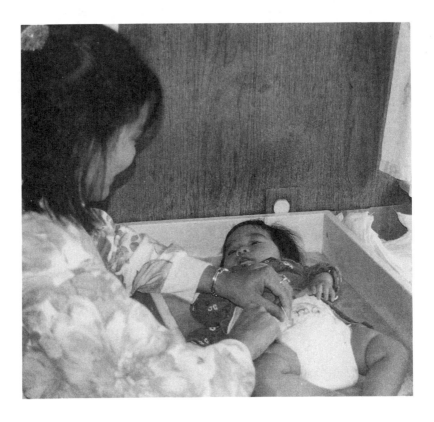

19. Diapering

HoW MANY TIMES DO YOU think a baby gets diapered? Six or seven thousand times. Why don't we do it nicely? Why don't we make it a learning experience? Why don't we want a child to enjoy being diapered?

Diapering is *very* important.

As a daily responsibility of parents and other carers of infants and toddlers, diapering is sometimes viewed as an unpleasant chore, a task of hygiene, a time separate from an infant's play and learning. But in the process of diapering, we should remember that we are not only doing the cleaning, we are intimately together with the child.

We are all affected, negatively or positively, by cumulative experiences in our lives. One of the first such cumulative experiences is diapering, involving much of the child's and parent's time and energy during those first, most impressionable two to three years of the child's life.

While being diapered, the baby is close to the parent and can see her face, feel her touch, hear her voice, observe her gestures, and learn to anticipate and to know her.

Diapering as a "Chore"?

A parent who perceives diapering as a chore will often develop a fast, efficient routine, with hygiene as the only goal in mind. Often, toys and rattles are put into the infant's hands to distract the baby's attention from the diapering activity. There is little eye contact or communication, since the parent concentrates on the lower part of the infant's body. And if the infant cries or objects, the parent often hurries even more, consoling the baby, "There, there, in no time we will be through, and then we can play together."

The outcome of this style of diapering is that it frequently becomes mechanical and depersonalized for efficiency's sake. The infant also may receive several negative messages, such as: that caring for the body and the body's processes are offensive, or that care activities are not enjoyable times together. When toys are given to an infant while he is being diapered, the baby is being encouraged to split his attention away from his body, away from the task at hand, and away from relating with his parent.

Diapering as Intimate Time Together

Diapering can be prime time for baby and parent, as enjoyable as playing together, when it is not seen as a chore. Within the process of diapering, there are many opportunities available for the infant in the form of learning experiences, playful interactions and the development of the parents' and infant's relationship.

The following sample dialogue illustrates the interaction and learning opportunities in an everyday encounter:

Carer	Infant	Learning Through
Greets child. "You seem to be having a good time with your rubber giraffe…"		Anticipation

80

Carer	Infant	Learning Through
Tells and shows what she is going to do. "…but I want to pick you up and diaper you."	Pays attention	Attention
Waits for infant's reaction.	Responds to the initiations of carer (positively or negatively)	Awareness
"You're not quite ready so I'll wait a little."	Pauses, looks at carer	Responsiveness to each other
… one or two minutes later …		
"Now you seem ready."		Expectations
"First we have to remove your overalls. You pull out your foot."	Cooperates and participates	The job of pleasing and of actively participating

Carer	Infant	Learning Through
"You helped with this (*touches foot*), now pull out the other foot."	Achieves mastery, becomes playful, teasing, doing the opposite of what is asked.[2]	Mastery
Enters the game but eventually gets back to task. "This (*smiling*) doesn't look like a foot, but more like a hand to me." *Enjoys the process.*	Enjoys the process, laughs	Joy of doing task together

These guidelines are not meant to create another style of "mechanized" diapering but to give you and your infant a sense of the importance of this daily care activity and to take fuller advantage of the many opportunities available for the infant through meaningful social, emotional, and physical exchange.

---

[2] Playful teasing by the infant (doing the opposite of what is asked or expected) indicates developing trust.

20. Feeding

FOR MOST NEW PARENTS, the most worrisome areas are crying, sleeping, and feeding/eating. Of course, they are interrelated.

Parents are often eager to give their babies the breast or a bottle whenever the babies show signs of any discomfort. For a new mother with a crying child, it can seem like a much too long-term project to find out why the baby is crying. The breast (or bottle) is available, and the crying stops right away. Nursing gives some mothers a good feeling, physically, and reassures them of their ability to know what the baby needs and that they are able to provide it. No wonder many people believe and advocate that the breast is the ideal comforter and soother—I do not.

Offering the breast is offering food. Food is what your baby needs when hungry. But to use food as a means to soothe, to overcome tiredness, to eliminate discomfort or pain, can create unhealthy habits for a whole lifetime.

Contrasting the simple physiological cycle of hunger/satiation with the complex psychological relationship we develop toward food helps us to a better understanding of parental attitudes and feeding problems.

The Physiological Cycle

Hunger/satiation is a physiologically determined rhythmic cycle, similar to ebb and flow. Nutrients are carried to the cells. The food supply diminishes in the stomach, and the brain sends hunger signals. Perceiving these signals as tension and discomfort, the infant cries, "asking" for food (relief). When given a breast or a bottle, the baby sucks, fills up, and gets satiated.

While infants vary in the amount of food they take at each feeding, the optimal goal should be to fill up the baby's stomach, allowing the baby to feel the sensation of fullness. Then, after time to digest the meal, the baby will gradually begin to feel the signs of hunger again.

A baby who has gotten into the habit of constant snacks may never experience real hunger nor real satiation and may develop a constant pseudo-need to suck and a continuous appetite for food.

Our Attitudes Toward Food

Eating is a necessity; it is also pleasurable. Food is used for a reward, for celebration, for consolation, for conditioning and for bribery. Food symbolizes love, mother, caring, happiness, social grace, relaxation, pleasure, satisfaction, and on and on. No wonder parents feel rewarded, accepted, and loved when their baby eats well and rejected when she does not—though the baby rejects only the food, not them.

Even if parents could divorce themselves from all that emotional overlay, feeding a baby is still an enormous responsibility. Parents usually have three major concerns: what to feed, when to feed (how often, for how long), and how to feed.

What and When to Feed

What to feed? We advise you to consult with your pediatrician. The advantages of breast feeding (natural protection, pleasurable for both, hygienic, easily available, no cost) are widely accepted. The benefits of bottle feeding and formulas are also well known (can be used by father and other carers, and you know how much the baby ate).

Breast-feeding mothers often ask: "Is my milk nutritious?" "Am I possibly eating something that is giving my baby colic?" and "Do I have enough milk?" The infant weight scale is a simple solution to some of these questions but is not widely used. Pediatricians do not recommend them, saying it makes parents more anxious to know how much, or maybe how little, babies eat. I cannot accept this thinking. Why would knowing make anybody more anxious than not knowing? I have never found it cumbersome to put a baby on a scale before and after each feeding. (The scale must be precise.)

To keep a diary on your baby's weight gains and the amount of food she consumes is the best way to learn about your baby's pattern of eating. Once you understand this pattern, it may be easier to see the changes and the relationship between food intake, crying and sleeping. You may also discover connections between some foods you eat and your baby's restlessness and crying.

When and how often to feed? Simple—when the baby is really hungry. But it is not easy to know when a baby is truly hungry. It will take you some time to differentiate a real hunger cry from others. It helps if you do not offer food as a first solution, but wait. Many babies stop crying all by themselves.

Remember, you can condition a baby to want food even when she is not hungry.

For how long should a baby eat? For as long as she is vigorously working on it. I do not believe that a baby should keep the nipple or bottle in her mouth while asleep, or while being distracted. Gently pulling the nipple out either reminds the baby that she is still hungry and stimulates her sucking, or allows her to let the nipple out easily if she is satiated. Most babies easily learn to suck all they need in a short period of time.

Where and How to Feed

Comfortable Position – Whether you breast- or bottle-feed, take your time to find the most comfortable position for yourself, as well as for the baby. I am saddened to watch how may parents feed in a hurry and in very poor positions. Why?

If your own body is fully relaxed, everywhere well supported, and you hold the baby so that you do not need to bend or tense, both of you will have a pleasurable time together (and for nursing mothers, your milk will flow more easily).

At home, it helps to feed at the same place. But wherever you do it, do make it comfortable.

Introducing New Foods – When to introduce new foods and what to offer should be discussed with your pediatrician, as there is a range of opinions.

Babies respond differently to new experiences such as a new food. When introducing a new taste, I would say, "Here is applesauce, you can try it." We offer the same new food for one or two weeks, once a day, never forcing it. If your baby turns her head away or shuts her mouth, you stop. She may taste tiny amounts before choosing to eat one quarter of a baby spoonful, and eventually she may even like the food. The child should like and enjoy the new foods we give her.

Do not be in a rush and do not push the baby.

Weaning – Weaning should be done in a very slow and gradual way according to the child's readiness. Eliminating one breast feeding at a time, keeping the morning and evening feedings as the last to go, continues these times of special closeness.

The process of weaning may not go smoothly, but in all parts of the world it is done sooner or later. Try to do it in harmony with the child, so he gets the food he enjoys and the nutrition he needs. Some children naturally go through this process faster than others.

Lap Feeding, then Small Table – Lap feeding offers opportunities for intimacy and a more comfortable position for infants than in a seat or high chair. I prefer babies to be fed in their parents' or carers' laps until they have matured enough to sit securely and to get in and out of their size-appropriate stool, bench or chair by themselves. The seat should be low enough for their feet to rest comfortably on the floor. True, it is easier to strap a toddler into a high chair than to help her learn to eat in her small chair; but we like the idea of teaching toddlers that, if they get up, this will be interpreted as a sign that they are not hungry, and so we take the food away. It is one of many ways of letting a child know that she has some control of how much she eats.

Three Spoons, Two Bowls – Most babies want to grab the spoon the adult is holding. We offer a different spoon to the baby. At first she will soon drop or throw it. Eventually, she will try to feed herself.

We make it a habit to have a larger bowl and a serving spoon with the whole food supply and a small bowl into which we put *tiny amounts* in front of the child. We feed the baby from the small bowl and also allow her to try to feed herself from this small bowl. (We refill from the larger one.)

As she becomes increasingly skillful in using the spoon, we let her eat more and more on her own, until we no longer use our spoon to help. This transition can take many months.

Changing Appetites – Parents easily get upset when a usually good eater becomes fussy. Remember that appetites change. A baby's need for food drops drastically around one year of age, when her rate of growth slows down, and also before and during an illness. If you do not coax and cajole, her appetite naturally comes back. With the two-spoon method of feeding, the tiny amounts of food in the smaller bowl will make the child eager to ask for more and you can give as many helpings as she asks for.

If you want your baby to develop a taste for wholesome food rather than junk food, have only nutritious food available.

Family Meals – Many parents ask whether babies should participate in family meals.

Family meals are very, very rarely pleasurable when babies are included. Not only do babies not have any table manners, they need constant attention, create a mess, and I cannot see why such a tense atmosphere is desirable.

I prefer that the parent feed a baby ahead of time (and maybe even for the baby to be in bed) by the time the parents enjoy a well-deserved, peaceful meal. When children can participate in table conversations, they are ready to join the family at the table.

Avoiding Feeding Problems

Our attitude toward food affects our physical and emotional health. Just think of the many people who struggle throughout life with eating and related problems, from overeating to anorexia, to drinking, smoking, and drug abuse.

Many of these problems could be avoided by remembering that:

- At no time, for no reason, should a child be forced, cajoled, talked or bribed into eating more than he wants to eat.

- When the child shows any disinterest, not even half an ounce nor a spoonful more should be offered. (This keeps the child's self-regulation intact.)
- Food should not be used as bribery or a reward. For instance, giving a baby a bottle so he will go to sleep confuses two of the most important primary needs. It can create both sleeping and eating difficulties.
- Wholesome food should be offered but the child's choices (tastes, likes, dislikes) respected.

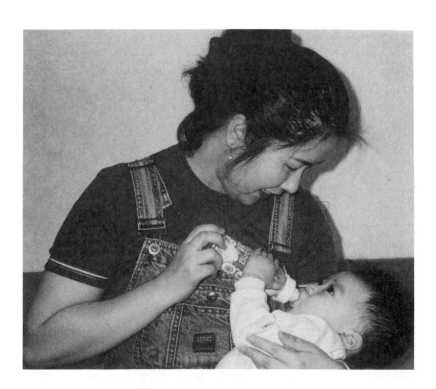

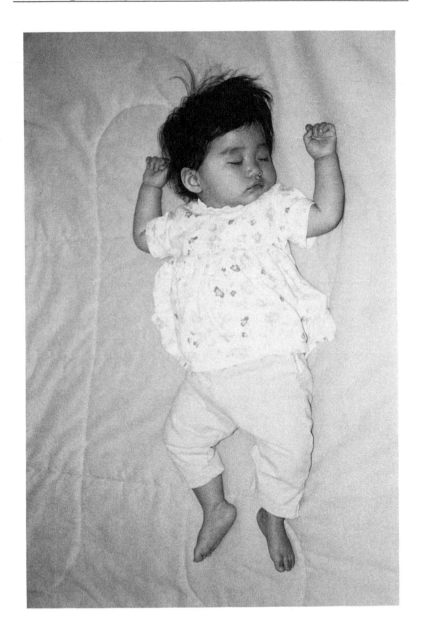

21. Sleeping

YOUNG CHILDREN ARE not asleep for eight hours and then awake all day, as most adults are. First, they fall asleep, then they wake up a little bit, then they fall asleep again.

Both the amount and the pattern of sleep change from child to child and, of course, change as a baby grows. Newborn and very young babies are asleep most of the time; they alternate periods of sleep and periods of wakefulness six to ten times within 24 hours, with an average of 18 to 21 hours of sleep. Two- to three-year-olds average 12 to 14 hours of sleep.

Everything that happens to your baby during the day can influence her sleep pattern. Young babies get tired often during the day, and if not distracted, would fall asleep. When parents complain about their babies' sleep patterns, they usually do not consider how their daily activities influence sleep.

Unfortunately in our busy society too few infants are given the opportunity to follow a natural, predictable daily routine. Often infants must adapt to the schedules of other members of the family. That means infants are not allowed to follow their biological clocks.

It is not easy for a family to juggle all duties without disrupting a baby's sleep-wake pattern.

Your goal is to help your baby develop good sleeping habits.

Developing Good Sleep Habits

The easiest way to develop good habits in general is to have a predictable daily life.

Does your baby spend plenty of time outdoors? (See, *Outdoor Living*, page 103) Building a room-size outdoor playpen is an excellent investment. Napping outdoors (protected from the sun) is a good habit.

Young babies thrive on routine. Ideally, daily events of eating, sleeping, bathing, outdoor play, etc., happen around the same time and in the same sequence each day. As the baby is learning to anticipate the next event, many conflicts are eliminated. A mutual adaptation of the biological rhythm of your baby and your family schedule develops. It also enables you, the parent, to plan for those blocks of time when your baby is usually napping or playing peacefully.

Recognizing Tiredness

I believe that you cannot go wrong letting children rest when they need it and giving them a very peaceful environment. After a slow-paced day, infants are more likely to sleep peacefully throughout the night.

Sensitively watch for the very first signs of tiredness (slowing down, closing eyes, being less focused, being irritable). That is the time an infant is ready for sleep. As time goes by, increased tiredness may build resistance—and once the "second wind" hits, going to sleep becomes an ordeal for both your baby and you. An overtired child sleeps restlessly, wakes up more often during the night, and gets up grouchy, too early in the morning.

Stress and overstimulation can also cause exhaustion, irritability and resistance to sleep.

Many parents I have advised have learned with surprise and

delight that, contrary to their fears, putting babies to bed very early in the evening did not make them wake up earlier in the morning. Indeed, their babies often woke up much later in the morning, adding hours of sleep.

Putting Your Baby to Bed

Parents often find that the easiest way to put their baby to bed is to give her a bottle or nurse her to sleep. I have observed, however, that as an infant becomes more aware of herself and of her environment, it is better to put her down while she is still somewhat awake. Waking up in a crib with no memory of having been put there can be disorienting and scary. Younger babies who are lifted into their cribs when asleep may wake up confused because of the sudden change (going from a more upright position to lying flat).

A Pre-Bedtime Ritual

As bedtime approaches, create an atmosphere that becomes progressively slower paced and more quiet. Do you happen to know the lovely book by Margaret Wise Brown, *Good Night Moon*, in which, page by page, the room darkens, gradually evoking a sleepy mood? This is the feeling I suggest you work toward.

Repeating a simple pre-bedtime ritual helps your baby to get ready gradually. For example, making a habit of commenting while putting away toys can be helpful: "The ball goes into this basket here in the corner; your doll sits on the top shelf; the toys will stay here until morning, when you can play with them again." Such comments build a bridge between "tonight" and "tomorrow" and provide a sense of continuity and security.

Then you may continue, "I am going to pull the curtains now, then I will turn off the big light and put on the night light, then I will go into the other room." As your infant grows older, she may take over the role and have such monologues herself.

Some infants have a special bed companion, a "lovey" such as a teddy bear or blanket (also referred to as a transitional object). Putting your child and her lovey to bed, you may talk to the bear, "Have a peaceful rest. I will cover both Alison and you so that the two of you will feel comfortable and cozy. Are you ready for your lullaby?" (You may want to sing or wind up a music box—a little music is a soothing way to end a day.) Finally, caress your baby gently and say, "Good night. I'll see you in the morning."

Falling, and Not Falling, Asleep

As you can see, I am giving you ideas of how you can create an atmosphere conducive to rest.

But remember, nobody can make another person fall asleep. How to relax and let sleep come is a skill your child, like everybody else, must learn all by herself.

Children also wake up several times during the night and learn how to ease themselves back into sleep (unless they have a need or get scared).

Some children seem to really need to cry themselves to sleep. Sometimes just letting them cry those extra parent-painful minutes before sleep can be helpful.

Theories and fads keep changing, from advising you to sleep together in the "family bed," to putting the infant far enough away not to be disturbed by his crying.

Be prepared that there will be times when a child may become reluctant to fall asleep: when she comes down with a sickness, shortly before a spurt of new development, or during certain vulnerable times of emotional growth (such as during the stage of separation anxiety).

Do not expect a magic formula; sometimes one problem area cannot be isolated from the rest of the everyday life of your baby.

Your overall attitude can make a difference. Do not feel sorry for "poor baby" who must go to bed—rather remember how good it feels to rest when you are tired, and how nice it feels to wake up refreshed.

Dorothy was much fussier and more dependent on me than my first child. It seemed she would never sleep, no matter how much I would nurse her, rock her, jiggle her or pat her, and she hated to be put down at all. I really felt at my wit's end; but I had read that some babies just need a lot more attention and comfort and a lot less sleep than others, and I guessed that's who Dorothy was.

It's hard for me to believe the transformation we've both gone through as a result of my taking Magda's class [at Pacific Oaks College]. To begin with, and despite my skepticism, I decided to try Magda's suggestion that babies spend some time playing on the floor. I put Dorothy on her back with a few toys near her. To my astonishment, rather than crying, she really enjoyed herself and in fact spent the first few times figuring how to roll over. I discovered that she could entertain herself.

Then I brought Dorothy with me to an all-day class, since I was uncomfortable leaving her at home for eight hours. Magda had all of us "observe" her, and I was so proud at how comfortable Dorothy seemed quietly playing, rolling, stretching, and reaching while we watched. I realized how much more delight I was finding in her, since learning to let her play on her own.

After about an hour, when Dorothy started to fuss mildly, I leaped to my feet, declaring that she was surely hungry, and nursed her for a few minutes. I put her down again, and a few minutes later she began to fuss again. Inside, I panicked. I just knew that unless I started major walking and jiggling she would get hysterical.

Magda gently asked me what I thought the problem was, and how I would solve it at home. I replied that I didn't know what the problem was, and at home I would pick her up. Magda then commented that to her, Dorothy seemed tired, and suggested that I wait a few minutes to see what happened. I waited, fully expecting a hurricane. Instead, first Dorothy moved her head back and forth a few times, then popped her fingers in her mouth, and fell asleep. It was the first time I had ever seen my child fall asleep on her own. My mouth was hanging open like a trap door.

Magda then suggested that falling asleep is a skill. While everyone learns it sooner or later (unfortunately, for a few, it is never easy without external—often pharmaceutical—aids), as parents we can best help our children to learn this skill by trusting that they can, and by refraining from the interference that conveys to them that they can't. I felt like one of those cartoon characters with a light bulb flashing over my head. Theory and application merged as I watched my daughter peacefully sleep through the rest of the morning class, soothing herself back to sleep when a noise disturbed her.

The next morning, when Dorothy started her tired fussing, I took her to her crib, explained calmly that she was tired, needed to sleep, and I couldn't do it for her, and left her. She slept for three hours and has been sleeping a lot ever since. No wonder the poor child was so cranky—she was exhausted.

22. Choosing
Play Objects

MANY PARENTS ARE CONCERNED about the hows, whys and whats of babies' toys.

First I would like to say that, rather than "toys," I prefer to call them play objects. We say that a baby is playing when she is manipulating an object (even if it is her own hand), so in fact any object a baby would choose to manipulate would be a play object.

Safety

As for my recommendations, the most important consideration is *safety*. Any play object must be safe for the infant who will use it.

This means a play object must be too big to be swallowed. A play object must not have removable parts. The eyes and ears of many teddy bears have ended up in babies' stomachs and, if they are lucky, in their stools. The peas and dried beans inside some stuffed animals can escape through tiny holes in the seams. (What a baby will typically do with these small, round objects is push them into his nose. The mucous inside the baby's nose can cause the bean to swell, and a doctor's help may be required to remove it.)

The small objects that older children play with (construction toys, tiny people and animals, etc.) are dangerous for infants and must be kept away from them. If you are in doubt about the swallowability of a toy, there is a size tester marketed for adults to use (available through educational supply houses and some big toy stores) that might be useful for you. Some people use the hollow core of a toilet paper roll to test a safe size: if the toy will fall through the cylinder, it is too small and should be kept away from babies.

Other elements of safety include checking a play object for sharp edges, breakability and anything that might cause suffocation. I would never give a baby a balloon for several reasons: for one thing, it might burst and frighten him; but more importantly, he might put a popped or unblown balloon into his mouth, get it caught in his throat and asphyxiate. For a similar reason I would not give an infant a silk or nylon scarf: babies tend to jam things into their mouths, and a flimsy fabric could cause a baby to choke.

I would also not give an infant any toy with liquid inside, such as those hourglass rattles with little beads floating in clear fluid. There is always the possibility that, if the rattle were to break, the beads could spill out; and since babies explore the world largely with their mouths, those beads could end up inside the baby.

Some of the loveliest toys to look at are ones I would not choose for use with groups of babies: those made of heavy wood. In a group situation a heavy wooden object may easily become a flying missile and may injure another child. However, for a single child at home, some wooden toys can be very nice.

I also do not like to see infants playing with objects that have long strings attached, such as pull toys for beginning walkers. The strings can too easily be wrapped around an infant's neck during normal play. (It is partly for these reasons that I do not recommend having infants and toddlers in the same group. Play objects and activities appropriate for toddlers can create an unsafe environment for infants.)

Recommendations

In general, play objects for babies should be simple, sturdy, and cleanable. In a baby's play space there should be a variety of sizes, shapes and weights represented (but none so heavy that a baby would be injured if she were to drop it). The arrangement of objects should be orderly; and the furnishings should be geared to the child regarding size, placement, etc.

Most importantly, play objects for infants need to be those which the infant can touch, grasp, look at, hold, mouth, and manipulate endlessly. It is easy to find such objects in your own kitchen or in a variety store.

First: A Scarf – If you have observed very young babies, you know how much they like to hold on to their blankets, clothing or diapers. I consider the best first "toy" a scarf about 18 inches square made of sturdy cotton or linen. (Never use flimsy material such as silk, nylon, etc.) You can buy or sew several in different colors and patterns. Hold the scarf in the middle and stand it up to form a peak. Place it at an angle where the infant can look at it, reach out for it, touch it and eventually grab it.

You will be amazed at how many different ways and for how long even a very young baby will manipulate such a scarf.

Containers – At RIE we have many plastic and other light weight containers for the babies to manipulate. Cups, bowls, colanders, dishpans and baskets in many sizes, shapes, and colors provide children with many hours of activity during their first two years of life.

Containers offer opportunities for babies to explore many notions, including "in" and "out," while the child remains in control of the activity and the object. This builds feelings of competence and confidence along with the concrete information gathered.

Collect a variety of colorful, sturdy plastic containers. Make sure some will nest inside others and that some will stack. Check to find some with which an infant can make interesting noises when tapping them against each other or the floor. Infants also enjoy holding things with holes in them, such as plastic bread baskets or colanders. Molded ice cube trays are a favorite, too. For more variety, include some lightweight, shiny metal plates or pans (but watch for sharp corners).

Balls – For all infants, I recommend balls, balls, balls: big ones, small ones, plastic whiffle-type ones with holes (babies love to put their fingers into the holes and move them around). I like beach balls blown up to different degrees of firmness, so it is easy for little fingers to grab and lift them. Rubber balls are fine (but not those made of rubber foam, as infants could bite and eat pieces). Inflatable water toys, especially beach rings, offer many different kinds of experiences for infants—all on dry land, of course.

Bottles, Chains – All sizes of empty plastic bottles, thoroughly cleaned, are safe, easy for babies to mouth, manipulate and safely poke their fingers into. They also make very interesting noises when they fall over or bump another object. The two-quart-size soda bottles are among the best of this type.

Plastic chains are always fascinating to infants. Those well-known large-sized pop beads are still favorites, as are newer types. Make sure, though, that if the chains are flexible, they are not long enough to tangle around a baby's neck or limbs. (This is not a concern with pop-type beads because the chain is not very bendable.)

Boxes – As a baby becomes older and more mobile, boxes of all types are excellent play objects. Large boxes can be crawled on, in or through; smaller ones can become containers for other play objects. Boxes can become towers, tunnels, walls, vehicles. Of course, the same criteria of safety and sturdiness hold for boxes as for other play objects.

Special Gifts – For something special that a child will use more as she becomes a little older, wooden toys are fine for one child to use at home. Many toy stores carry beautiful wooden blocks and lovely wooden puzzles of simple shapes with knobs for little fingers to lift each piece. Dolls (safe, with no small, removable parts) and some preschool materials, such as wooden cylinder sets in their own trays, make fine gifts.

Active Infant, Passive Object

What do all of these recommended play objects have in common? None *do* anything. They will respond only when the infant activates them. In other words, our *active* infant manipulates *passive* objects.

In contrast, entertaining kinds of toys (such as mobiles or, later on, wind-up toys or battery-operated items) cause a passive infant to watch an active toy. This trains the child to expect to be amused and entertained and sets the scene for later TV watching. I dislike toys labeled "educational," especially for the first year of life. (See, *Equipment: What Is Really Necessary?*, page 159)

The best materials for infants need not be fancy, but neither are they limited to cast-offs. The best play objects are those which allow infants to be as active and competent as possible at every stage of development.

23. Outdoor Living

BABIES THRIVE OUT-OF-DOORS. They sleep better, eat better, look better, play better, and learn better. Fresh air both soothes and stimulates. I always tell parents how much more easily they could raise healthy, "happy" children if they would make outdoor living a regular habit for their babies.

Very young babies will sleep much of the time; but as they grow older, they learn to enjoy being outdoors, spending time sleeping, eating, playing, just as they would do indoors.

Your Infant's Outdoor Play Area

If possible, establish an outdoor play area for your baby. An ideal situation would be to live in a fairly pollution-free area with direct access to a fenced-in yard with grass and trees, or to a porch, patio, etc. In my experience, when you have to carry out a crib or playpen every day, or several times a day, it just gets to be too much. If you have such a space, make the best investment and buy, perhaps secondhand, a duplicate crib or playpen[3] to keep outdoors. (See, *Equipment: What Is Really Necessary?*, page 159).

Like most activities in daily life with baby, whatever gets done regularly and routinely gives predictability and security to both

---

[3]   A playpen should have a bottom part made of wood, a firm water proof pad, and a cotton cover on top. (It is not pleasant to have a naked body in direct contact with plastic.)

baby and parent.

As the infant becomes more mobile, the size of his outdoor play area should be increased. Ideally, he should have a very *large* playpen (small room size) in which to roll and crawl and eventually creep. After 12 to 18 months, a part of the yard (large room size) should be fenced around. Eventually a safe, fenced-in yard may become the child's territory.

Starting Out Outdoors

A healthy full-term newborn can be taken out at about four weeks of age—at first, only when the temperature outside is similar to the one in the infant's room. Keep him dressed or covered the same way he is indoors. Keep the crib in the shade, and take the infant out preferably after feeding and diapering. Probably he will fall asleep.

Starting with about 15 minutes first, you can increase the timing each day. When your baby becomes three months or older, many of his waking hours can be spent outdoors.

Sun and Weather

To expose very young children to direct sun can be dangerous. A baby who is sleeping outdoors should stay in the shade. An umbrella or towel can be used to provide shade and adjusted to change as the sun's rays move. By the time the baby plays in a playpen, he can be naked! (Sunscreen is recommended.) Being outdoors in the morning is safer, midday sun should be avoided.

It doesn't matter what season of the year it is, especially in moderate climates. But of course, too much sun, too strong and rapid changes of temperature, extreme cold, extreme heat, dense fog, heavy smog, strong winds, etc., should all be avoided. You must use your judgment and, of course, dress the baby appropriately. In many countries, children do get accustomed to, and enjoy, very cold weather. They sleep on terraces under protected roofs while it rains—even snows—outside.

Frequent Checking

When your baby is outside, you should keep checking on her. Ideally, stay at hearing and seeing distance; but you can still go on with your own activities. Do not let your baby cry outside. Try to guess what started the crying in the first place and, if possible, attend to it. Stay out a little while with your baby; and if the crying continues, take her inside. But by all means take the child out again later. Probably it just was not the right time.

Benefits

If you start at an early age, your baby will learn to love the outdoors and will enjoy herself there. These times will help her be less inclined to be clingy, nagging, overly dependent, constantly needing company or entertainment.

The stimuli which nature provides are unparalleled. Even the youngest infant becomes fascinated by listening to the birds, watching the movements of flies, butterflies, shadows and leaves. Air circulation, temperature change, the playfulness of sunlight and shadow are strong stimuli to the skin, the eyes, the lungs, and the metabolism. As the young organism learns to adjust to and cope with constant changes, it becomes more resistant.

Of course, the child can also have toys in the play area or yard. But what a different learning experience your child will have watching nature, rather than watching TV!

24. Discipline: Clarifying the Goal

CHILDREN NEED EXPECTATIONS. They need to know where they stand in all kinds of life situations. They need to know the rules.

Discipline is an integral part of this rooted, secure feeling. From birth on, the parent sets the life-space for the child. At RIE, we certainly believe in the benefits of discipline, for both parents and infants.

The word discipline has different meanings, both according to the dictionary and in people's minds. Take a moment to close your eyes and mentally clarify how *you* feel about discipline. Open your eyes and write down your own definition of it.

Parents often think of it as punishment, corporal or otherwise, or as a system of punishments and rewards. I see discipline as being a social contract in which family or community members agree to accept and obey a particular set of rules. (See, *"House Rules,"* page 111)

You may be surprised, as I was, after reading this dictionary definition of discipline: *"Training that develops self-control, character."*

If one would think of what is to be accomplished, what is to be achieved by discipline, there would be an entirely different feeling for what it is. With discipline, you must have a certain goal in mind.

A positive goal to strive for when disciplining would be to

raise children we not only love, but in whose company we love being. This is not easy to do. Basically, most parents are afraid of disciplining their children because they are afraid of the power struggle. They are afraid of overpowering the child, afraid they will destroy the child's free will and personality. This is an erroneous attitude.

Discipline is not a goal in itself. It serves the reality of living within a society. Lack of discipline is not kindness, it is neglect.

Sometimes it is very difficult and even painful to discipline. It is easier to say, "Yes, okay, have your own way." But then what has been accomplished?

Realistic Expectations

One misconception most parents share is that children must be happy all the time. That is an unrealistic expectation because there are instinctual desires that we have but cannot satisfy at a given moment, or maybe ever. Life is a combination of pain and pleasure.

Young children cry when they cannot have what they want. Parents sometimes so identify with their infant and his tears that they cannot bear denying him his heart's desire.

But it is not the best thing to try to keep your children happy all the time. That is not the way life is. Getting to many goals involves struggle and sometimes pain. That is the human condition. When children find this out too late, after being sheltered and buffered unrealistically, they may find it difficult and frightening to cope with real life.

There is no way over-indulged children are going to be happy, because they seldom get direct, honest responses from their parents. These parents are basically negligent.

Saying "No"

It is not always easy for parents to say "No."

A parent's ambivalence, guilt feelings, and areas of confusion in his or her role will be picked up and used amazingly fast by young children. They seem to have a sixth sense for it. Any ambivalence from a parent will produce a nagging response.

Know what is important, both for you and for the infant. If you are not clear, the infant's opposition will persist, which will make you, the parent, even angrier. This in turn highlights the conflict that exists already, leading to an unhappy situation combining anger, guilt, and fear. A child has a difficult time growing up with ambivalent parents.

Children *need* discipline and structure. Be clear. Be honest. When you say "No," really mean it. Let your face and posture reflect "No" as well.

Learning for a Lifetime

Once the external disciplinary lessons are learned, the child begins to internalize—to learn the lessons on his own—and even realize that some things that are desired are not always good for us or for others.

Structure, expectations, predictability—all add to responsibly raising and loving our children. The freedom we all feel deep within ourselves comes once we understand where we stand in the scheme of things.

25. "House Rules"

LIVING WITHIN A SYSTEM of generally accepted rules makes life easier for all of us.

While rules vary among cultures and among families, I think most people would agree that a mutually acceptable system of rules is helpful for coexistence. This system can be determined within each family by clarifying the needs of its members and then developing a set of rules or guidelines which accommodates those needs as much as possible. After deciding on the rules, a parent must then introduce them to the child and reinforce them.

The question is "How?" My guidelines for the "how" are as follows:

- Establish a few, simple, reasonable rules and make sure they are age-appropriate;
- Expect these rules to be obeyed;
- Be consistent but not rigid;
- Give the child choices within a secure framework;
- Remember that even children (*especially* children) need to be able to save face and avoid power struggles.

Simple, Age-Appropriate Rules

First of all, remember that discipline is not a set of rigidly enforced mandates, but a process in which the infant learns to become a social being. Social learning, like any other form of learning, is dependent upon the child's readiness. Don't expect things of an infant that are against the very nature of her current developmental stage. To expect a newborn not to cry, a very young baby not to put things in her mouth, or a toddler not to say "no" is unreasonable. Also, timing is important. One cannot expect cooperation from a sleepy or hungry baby.

Expectations

In my practice I have seen that a child's response to parental demands depends very much upon the parents' own deep-down expectations. The way a demand is expressed triggers the child to do something or not to do it. If the parent does not really believe in the validity of a particular rule, or is afraid that the child will not obey, chances are the child will not.

An ambivalent parent will make things more difficult. Know your role as a parent. You must have certain goals and principles for your children. (See, *Discipline: Clarifying the Goal*, page 107)

Consistency

Predictability is habit-forming. Developing habits makes it much easier to live with rules.

Because very young children do not understand the reasons behind the rules they are expected to follow, it is better if these rules become simply a matter of course. There are some things we do not need or want to re-examine every time we do them, such as brushing our teeth. It is much more convenient for us if actions like these become habits.

In addition, we all know how difficult it is to change habits once we have them. For this reason alone, we should try to establish good habits from the very beginning. This is why I tell parents to start creating patterns and routines right from the child's birth. (See, *Predictability: Helping Your Child Feel Secure*, page 57) For example, it is much easier to get a baby to go to sleep when the same routine precedes each night's bedtime. This should continue until the *child* herself indicates the need for some sort of change.

Through regularity of routines, babies eventually learn to anticipate that which is expected of them. This is the beginning of discipline.

Choice Within Boundaries

Boundaries which are predictably and consistently reinforced provide security. In order to really develop inner discipline, children must be given the freedom to make choices. Knowing when to give infants freedom and when to introduce limits is most important and is the backbone of the RIE approach.

We need to remember that limits function as traffic signals, keeping things flowing smoothly between family members. Within this framework are those things a child is expected to do (non-negotiable areas), what she is allowed to do (negotiable areas), what is tolerated ("I don't really like that, but I can understand why you need to do it") and what is forbidden ("I don't want you to do that"). These are the parameters of discipline.

Within these parameters are what I perceive as important areas of choice. Babies must have freedom in the area of gross motor development and play. Parents provide safe, appropriately sized rooms or fenced areas in which the infants can move and explore freely, and parents provide safe and simple play objects— but the infants choose how they want to move and to learn. The infants' use of objects and play materials should not be restricted or interfered with.

Avoiding Power Struggles

If a child has ample opportunity to play independently, without interruption, he is likely to be much more willing to cooperate with the demands of his parent. One can further enhance the child's sense of himself as a decision-maker by allowing enough time to elapse after requesting something, so that the child can decide on his own whether or not to cooperate.

And we must understand that children need to be able to save face when they have not obeyed a rule. Young children fight an inner struggle. One part of them wants to please, yet they also have to resist in order to test the limits of their power. (See, *Quality Time*, page 75) In a way, each one of us carries around that eternal two-year-old, who shouts "No!" as he is offered an ice-cream cone, even while reaching for it. Most of us seldom like to be told what to do, even when it is good for us.

Teaching and Reinforcing Rules

In our RIE parent-infant classes[4] a demonstrator models how we teach and reinforce rules. As babies become young toddlers and can sit by themselves, we offer a snack at a special table around which the demonstrator and the toddlers sit. The snack is always predictably the same: bananas and diluted apple juice. Toddlers may choose to eat or not to eat, but they may not take food or juice away from the table.

It is an incredible learning experience for all of us to see how even the youngest toddlers at the table learn the rule and decide whether or not to obey it. After many repetitions of the rule, they get the message and then have to test it over and over again.

---

[4]   These classes meet for two hours once a week. (See, *About RIE*, page 191)

We've often seen a toddler steal away from the table and then turn back to make sure that the demonstrator sees her, as though she were checking to see whether the rule would be enforced. This shows that the child "understands" that a rule exists.

It is natural for toddlers to want to carry food away from the table; they can see no real reason not to. When a child ignores the rule, the demonstrator tries to show that she fully understands the child's desire to do what he wants and that he is not naughty or bad for having that desire. Therefore, she does not get angry with the child but calmly repeats the rule as she enforces it.

Of course, parents get irritated after their toddlers test rules repeatedly. But the child's behavior may become easier to handle once one realizes that it stems from a natural inclination and not from a desire to drive the parent crazy. (See, *Toddlers*, page 137)

Understanding and Mutual Respect

Children, like adults, need rules and guidelines. The RIE approach to discipline is based on understanding and mutual respect among family members, and it facilitates these qualities as well. We could easily exchange the word "discipline" for the word "Educaring"; they are both a combination of learning and nurturance. The goal is inner or self-discipline, self-confidence, and joy in the act of cooperation.

26. Praise or Acknowledgment

SINCE WE VALUE INNER-DIRECTEDNESS in a child, we prefer to offer gentle validations instead of instructions, criticism, and even praise.

Occasional reflections reassure the infant of our full attention and show our empathy. Rather than to give praise, the adult can be a "broadcaster" and describe the child's actions.

"You touched the ball, and it rolled away."

"It's hard to separate the two cups."

"Jonathan is standing up all by himself!"

A joyful smile when the infant solves a problem conveys our pleasure in his success.

By being quietly available, appreciating and enjoying what the infants actually do, we reinforce their self-initiated activities.

Acknowledging Positive Behavior

I prefer giving acknowledgment, rather than rewards.

"I like it when you pick up your toys."

Do not promise a reward for behavior that you can expect of your young children—let them know how good you feel about them. Just seeing the beaming smile of admiration on his parent's face is rewarding enough for an infant.

Whereas most people respond to negative behavior, we try to emphasize positive behavior. We prefer to give attention to the infant at the times we see behavior we would like to encourage.

The commonly used "good girl" or "good boy" often becomes mechanical and is subtly demeaning. It implies a child's value as a person is contingent on his "performance." It can create a conflict for the child. He may think he is "bad" if he acts differently from whatever has just been praised as "good."

Children don't need big hooplas, just a strong acknowledgment on your part.

Criteria for Praise

I do have a few criteria for praise:
- Do not praise a child who is happily playing;
- Do not praise a child who is "performing" for adults;
- Praise a child for social adaptation—for doing things that are very difficult, like waiting or sharing.

27. Opposing Needs, Different Points of View

CONFUSION OVER DISCIPLINE often arises during those in-between, "negotiable" situations which frequently occur between parents and their infants—for example, when your child wants you to be with him at the moment you want to do something else. Should you sacrifice your moment for your baby's demands, or is that not realistic just then?

The answer is seldom a simple formula. Living together with others involves understanding different points of view.

If the goal is a better relationship, a more peaceful living together, then it helps to learn a whole new attitude, a whole new way of understanding your infant, yourself, and the conflict of needs.

Respecting Your Own Needs

It helps to be strongly attuned to your own inner rhythm—to know what your needs are, and to convey this to your family so they learn to respect your needs, too. Ongoingly sacrificing your own needs for the child's can create inward anger within both of you.

If it is important that you finish reading the newspaper before you play with your young child, then clearly convey that message. Let her know what it is you want to do for yourself and what you expect her to do, so that playing quietly while you read can later grow into longer stretches of secure separateness, with both of you doing something independent of the other and still feeling good about your relationship.

"Switching" to the Infant's Point of View

Learning to "switch" to another person's point of view can help you as a parent and a person now and in the future. What makes this approach difficult with infants is that the adult is the only one who does the switching. You must be able to see and understand both your child's and your own "points of view." This is the role of the parent. Very young children cannot yet do it, and some children never learn to see a situation through their parents' eyes.

I will give you an example. After spending many hours peacefully with your eight-month-old Ryan, you would like to visit with your friend on the phone. Ryan, who had looked peacefully absorbed, stops playing and starts screaming. You feel it is unfair. Have you not just spent leisure "quality time" with him?

Now, try to switch to Ryan's point of view. He does not have the capacity to think, "My mommy gave me so much attention for so long, she now needs time for herself." All he feels is, "I want her, and she is not here."

Would it be good, then, for you to stop doing anything for yourself and only consider what Ryan wants? Many "good" mothers try to do just that, until their resentment of their babies becomes so strong that it scares them. Resentment does not help any relationship, least of all between parent and child.

If you switch back to your own point of view, you can tell your son, "I know you would like me around you" (acknowledging his point of view), "but I want to talk on the phone now" (validating your own feelings). "I'll be back with you in twenty minutes" (giving him hope).

Of course, Ryan will still want you to do nothing else but be available to him. Remind yourself that nobody can or even should have everything they want whenever they want it. So, do not feel sorry for him. Nor does it help to get angry with him. Learning to wait, not always to have your own way, is a difficult task—part of the curriculum of early childhood. The more mature capability of switching points of view is the task of parents. In the process, parents learn to assess sensitively both their babies' needs and their own needs and how to balance them.

The first time I took my son to RIE, I was struck by the encouragement we got as parents to make sure we got our needs met. Magda would encourage us to respect ourselves, as we respected our child. Learning this has been difficult at times, since all around us our experience is that we "should" sacrifice for our child(ren)!

Recently at a birthday party I realized how much RIE had really changed my life. The children had finished eating quickly and had resumed playing, while the adults were eating lunch and visiting with each other. Halfway through the meal my friend's son approached her and asked her to go with him and play the game with the other children. Looking down at her plate, my friend (who is very attentive to her child) tapped her fork on her salad, put it down, got up and left the table to accompany the child to the play area.

I stopped, started to stay something, and realized she was gone. I was surprised at her reaction. Perhaps if I hadn't heard and been encouraged so often by Magda to take care of myself also, I might have jumped up to please my child, too. Instead, I could hear myself saying, "I'm eating now, and you'll have to wait until I am finished." What RIE has helped me to do is "internalize" that my basic needs are important, too. It's okay to finish eating; it's okay to take my shoes off, change my clothes, and go to the bathroom before I change that diaper. The payoff for me is that some of my needs are met, and I can then give back to my child without resentment or anger. My child eventually learns to respect my needs and those of others, while learning to respect himself.

28. Adapting to New Developments

As BABIES GROW and develop, they also change, and the changes disrupt the previous status quo. Throughout the life cycle, we go through sensitive periods during which we are more vulnerable to certain situations than at other times. The first few years of life are filled with continuing cycles of disequilibrium— adaptation—harmony. For parents, it means continually adapting to new developments.

Knowing what you *can* realistically expect at given stages of your child's development may make it a little easier to understand the difficulties of separation and stranger anxiety, the "No! No!" period, sudden loss of appetite, sleep disturbances, toilet training and other times of change.

The most important thing to remember is that changes in your child's behavior are not "setbacks" but are simply part of her ongoing growth and development.

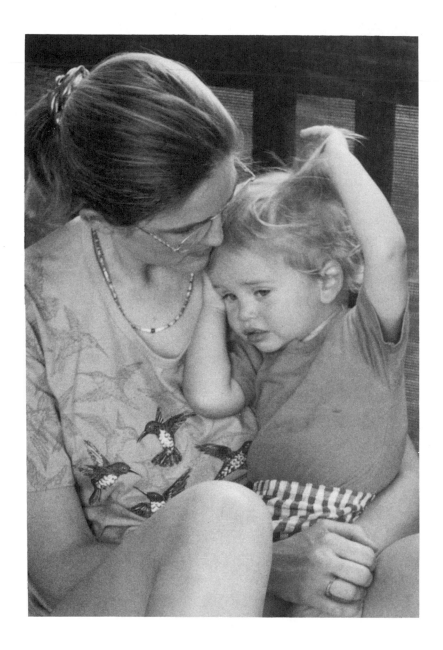

29. Separation and Stranger Anxiety

A TIME OF EQUILIBRIUM follows the newborn stage, as most babies begin to look plump and glowing. They start to move and explore peacefully for extended periods and seem to learn new skills with incredible speed all by themselves. You think you've made it.

Then, in the latter part of the first year, your peaceful baby may suddenly start screaming at a visitor, crying when you leave the room, and clinging to you desperately. What did you do wrong, you wonder?

Nothing. Baby is developing, becoming more aware of himself as a separate human being and of you, too, as a separate human being. He has learned to know and recognize his parent. He has learned that he cannot always make you magically appear whenever he wants you. This, like many other new discoveries, can be frightening. It is called separation anxiety. What to do about it?

If you have followed the RIE approach from the beginning, you have always told your baby when you left her, even when she was just a few weeks old. ("I'll just go to the bathroom. I'll be right back," or "I'm going to the kitchen for about 20 minutes," or "I'm going away for a few hours and then I'll come back. Grandpa will stay here with you.") Now it is even more important to inform your baby, even though you are pretty sure she will protest.

What makes separation difficult for your baby is that she is always the one "left." This may make her feel deserted and powerless. To help her experience that she has some control and to feel more powerful during separation, I suggest you create situations in which the baby is the initiator, the active problem-solver. You could go to a park, make a "home base" by putting a blanket, a basket, or diaper bag on the ground and sitting down. Once your child feels reassured that you are staying put, she may move away from you a little, then come back, then go off again—exercising her ability to separate from you.

Stranger Anxiety

During this period, your baby may also display "stranger anxiety"—a fear of others (even people she has known before, such as a relative who visits once in a while) or of new places, new situations, etc. She may seem distressed when "well-meaning" people come too close, pat or touch her. If this happens, simply say to the person, "Please don't move too close. Just wait; my daughter does not know you and may be afraid of you."

A Vulnerable Time

Interestingly, it often happens at the peak of the child's separation anxiety that even the most devoted parents feel like getting away from their child. This is understandable because at this time children are more fussy and clingy. While I understand the parents' needs, I still suggest that they postpone their vacation plans until the child feels more secure. This is a most vulnerable time and is not a good period for parents to leave; it would only reinforce these fears.

It is not easy for parents to go through their children's emotional stages of attachment and separation anxiety. But while all young children go through these difficult times, it is much easier for those infants who have had the opportunity to explore their own play area freely, both with and *without* anybody in it. (Another argument for that safe space! See, *Time Apart: A Space for Your Baby,* page 15)

30. Sharing and Conflicts

BEFORE A CHILD CAN learn to share, she needs to go through certain stages of development.

In the beginning an infant perceives herself not as separate, but as part of the world she feels, touches, tastes, sees, and hears. Slowly an awareness emerges that there is a separate world outside, that there is a "me" and a "non-me." Later she realizes that there are differences in people, there is a "Mommy" and a "not Mommy," and there are familiar and non-familiar people and objects. At this stage, when a child holds or even just wants an object, in her mind it is "hers." The child does not yet have the concept of ownership.

Sharing is based on the knowledge of ownership and use. The owner lets someone else use an object with the knowledge that it will be returned later. But the infant has no concept of time. Only "now" exists. Even two minutes may seem like forever. We cannot expect a young child to perceive what sharing means.

If we expect behavior from our young children that they are not ready for or do not understand, then even if they do what we ask, it will be done because they feel parental pressure, a desire for parental approval, or out of fear of punishment.

Personality characteristics such as generosity, empathy, caring and sharing cannot be taught—but they can be learned through experience. Growing up in a family where parents share not only objects, but also time and attention, will help an infant to develop these personality traits later.

Dealing with Conflicts

There are certain behaviors that we *can* expect of our children. If your child is hurting another child, for example, you should be firm. You are in charge, and you cannot allow any child to hurt another.

With young infants, who are exploring by mouthing or pulling hair or trying to touch eyes, I just do a little bit of gentle monitoring: "Yes, you can touch, but touch easy—and not the eye." I give the message of gentleness or easiness.

Later, when it is much more volitional, I say, "No, I don't want you to do that," very simply.

With a group of toddlers (up to six—more than this will make a crowd who cannot be expected to enjoy each other's company), it helps to have several of the same toys available. Of course, a child will always want the truck that the other child is playing with because it is moving, it is "alive."

If you see a conflict developing, you can do the following:

- First, move peacefully, stay close, and wait patiently. The children may be able to handle it themselves. If the children are struggling without harming each other, it is good practice for them and they should be allowed to continue.
- You could then state the conflict in a non-judgmental way, by making a comment such as, "Both you, Andrea, and you, Jason, want the same truck." This helps calm the children by letting them know that you understand and empathize with their situation.
- If they are still in conflict, you may look around the

room and ask the children if they see another toy they would like to play with. (Picking it up and playing with the toy yourself may make it attractive to the toddler.)

- If the conflict continues, you may choose to inter-vene. You might put away the toy in question. In other words, *you* facilitate peace and quiet, handle the conflict, and resolve the situation instead of letting the children continue to struggle.

Following the RIE approach, we start with the least amount of help and intervention and then slowly increase it. We do expect and trust that even infants eventually learn most by working out conflicts all by themselves. If every time adults jump in and bring in their version of what is right, the children learn either to de-pend on them or to defy them. The more we trust they can solve, the more they do learn to solve.

Magda has always said, "When we make a child share, it is not sharing." This is a difficult concept for most of us, and yet I have found that when I have given the children a choice to share or not to share, with no repercussions, their inner-directed responses tend to be far more generous and giving.

It's very difficult to watch children tug at a toy, scream and struggle—without intervening. Yet as I did so, I was surprised to see how quickly these conflicts blew over. The children worked through it and soon were busy doing something else. They had a chance to feel and express their real feelings, learn to experience the consequences in the real world, and move on.

31. Biting

CHILDREN WHO BITE ARE problems for many families and real trouble in group settings.

Our reactions and remediation would be different depending on the age of the child, the frequency of the biting, the situation in which it occurs and the basic well-being and mood of the child (whether the child seems reasonably happy, or irritable much of the time).

Younger Infants

The problem usually begins when the peacefully nursing mother first gets bitten by her suckling infant. A surprised "ouch" and withdrawal of the breast lets the baby know that she does not like to be bitten.

Infants first bite because biting comes naturally, because their gums are itchy and their teeth are coming in.

Like mouthing, biting is instinctual. Erik Erikson describes it as the oral-aggressive phase of infancy. Because it is instinctual, adults respond to it with more anger, anxiety and vengeance than to other aggressive acts. Outbursts such as "I'll bite you back so you'll feel how it hurts" or "Don't you bite ever again!" are common. The absurdity of the demand, "Don't you bite ever again!" was terrifyingly illustrated by a little autistic child who indeed stopped biting altogether and changed his normal eating habits into swallowing only pureed food.

Toddlers

While in early infancy biting is rather exploratory, toddlers bite when frustrated, angry or tired. Young children want what they want right away with no delay. This is the very nature of childhood. Waiting can be too upsetting. With this type of biting, I say, firmly, "No," and "I don't want you to bite, and I won't let you bite."

Sometimes frustration builds up over a period of time. Young children may become irritable because their basic needs are not met properly. Too much stimulation or poor timing may interfere with their biological rhythm, preventing them from sleeping when sleepy or eating when hungry. Parents may have difficulty coordinating their own activities to provide a predictable environment for the baby. If a child shows other signs of frustration, I would look at his daily life to discover the source of his overall maladjustment and change it.

Chronic Biting

If I have to deal with a child who often bites and who intimidates other children, I must use sensitive but strong strategy. Not only are the other children afraid of the biter, the biter may be even more afraid of his own potential power to harm. Both "victim" and "aggressor" need to feel that the adult is in charge and can protect them.

Years ago at RIE there was a two-year-old child who was notorious for biting. His mother was desperate. She said that as soon as the children saw her son, Andy, on the playground, they ran away from him.

Andy and four other children came once a week for two hours to our infant program. When I first saw Andy bite, I told him calmly but firmly, "I will not let you bite any child or big person. If you feel like biting, here are things (teething rings, rubber or plastic objects, etc.) you can bite."

From then on I watched him very closely in order to predict what would trigger his desire to bite so that I could prevent him from doing it. When I sensed he was getting out of control, I would hold him firmly but not punitively, telling him that I would not let him bite. (I think that this allowed him to learn to trust me). He eventually relaxed and I let go of him.

At times Andy playfully chewed on a plastic donut, part of a stacking toy. Once Andy got upset and started to run. Lo and behold, another child inadvertently crossed his path. This was too much for Andy, and he bit her. I said to Andy, "I saw you wanted to get your ring, but it was too far and Tammy got in your way. How about attaching your ring to your shirt, so you will have it right there when you need it?" Andy was so proud of his own biting ring that all the other children asked to have one, too. This lasted for a little while and was the end of any biting in that group.

This anecdote is an account of one way of dealing with a problem. However, this should not be used as a "what to do" solution, but rather as how to apply the basic principle of working on problems *with* nature, not against it.

32. Toddlers

Toddlerhood is a time of constant struggle.

For the child, it is a period of strong ambivalence. He is filled with turmoil and overwhelming opposite feelings. No suggestion you give will be right, because a toddler has opposing inner needs of his own. He needs to feel dependent *and* independent, big *and* little, strong *and* weak. At various times, the toddler feels omnipotent and helpless.

As a child becomes upright and starts to toddle, as he begins to understand language, the sense of security he achieved during his first year or so of life is shattered. He is able to sense more and more about the human condition, about reality. As he begins to acquire language, he becomes able to communicate his needs. No longer is he the dependent, cuddly baby who elicits compassion, love and caring. Instead he is an explorer. He must find out who he is and how much power he has.

Toddlers have an exuberant feeling about themselves but they don't yet have the judgment about what they really can and cannot do. They are also afraid of their own power, so at this stage they need freedom, but guidance—lots of guidance.

Once you understand the importance and magnitude of your child's struggle, your attitude can begin to support his rapid physical and emotional growth.

It is difficult to live with a toddler with focus and empathy.

The toddler is a terrible, terrific, tiresome, true, torn human being. There are times when he believes he owns the world; and at other times, he believes all the world is his enemy.

You need enormous amounts of *energy, patience,* and *compassion.*

You must try to learn what is the *optimal* distance to keep from him while he is exploring. You can learn to function as an island of security in the sea of confusion and anxiety.

You may be able to communicate a feeling of security to your child if you yourself can inwardly believe that this crucial period is really very short, even though it seems to last forever.

And most of all, you need *humor.*

To live with a toddler can, in a funny way, be therapeutic. All the human anxieties—of feeling good and bad, loved and abandoned—peak. It is like a ritual of passage in the journey as a family. If this passage from babyhood to "pre-schoolness" was difficult for you as a child, it may be difficult for you to go through again. Eventually in our journey as parents, we may have to explore the scary things of our own childhood. We may try to avoid this opportunity or view it as therapeutic.

33. Toilet Training

TOILET TRAINING IS a natural process. All normal people learn it. Different societies have different methods, but the important thing is readiness.

The reality is that once a child is ready and decides to use the toilet, he knows how to do it. It is unnecessary to teach, practice, or exercise the little techniques often suggested to parents.

Children gradually learn what they need to know if parents encourage cooperation whenever they care for their children. If diapering has been a pleasurable experience, a true dialogue between parent and child—if caregivers give full attention during these times—there may be no need for special training.

Exuberant praise, rewards, bribes, and reprimands are not only unnecessary, but manipulative. Psychologically, they can deprive a child of making this important step towards autonomy of his own volition.

In order to convey my concerns, I want to emphasize how much more is involved in learning to use the toilet than just getting urine and feces into the toilet.

Such learning happens as a result of a healthy, normal child, living in an average accepting, caring family. As part of his natural development the child wants to be like, and act like, his parents. The child has to be ready *physically* (have the capacity of the bladder to hold more fluid, better muscle control), *cognitively* (be fully aware of what he is expected to do), and *emotionally* (be ready and willing to give up a comfortable situation, such as just letting out urine and feces in diapers whenever it happens naturally).

For the child, it means that he has to delay and control a natural urge; to give away something that he may believe is still part of his body, and therefore valuable; and to conform to an adult-designed and timed routine. This may be a time of inner conflict.

Endless volumes have been written on toilet training. Without going into more detail on this huge subject, I will mention some of the struggles of early childhood which have an effect throughout our life:

- dependence or independence and autonomy,
- taking or giving,
- holding on or letting go,
- progression (wanting to grow up) or regression (wanting to stay a baby).

Though these are lifelong struggles, they seem to be crucial during this stage of development.

Dear parent, trust your child.

Remember the importance of every experience in the long process of learning.

For my youngest, diaper changing, bathing, feeding and dressing were special times. There was no struggle over toilet training. Between two and two-and-a-half, she decided she was ready and trained herself. I gave her the choice of using the adult toilet with a step stool or a potty chair.

My son's biggest recent accomplishment is his new toileting ability. At age three-and-a-half, he decided to learn to use the toilet and, within a week, he had mastered both toileting skills by himself. He still "announces" his use of the facilities but is very competent at this skill.

Our daughter has been using the toilet competently for some time now with no "training" whatsoever. We just got her a child's toilet (one small enough for her feet to touch the floor) long before she was ready to use it, and told her that this was her own toilet to use when she wanted. A long time passed before she even attempted to use it, and it was several more months before she had completed all the stages of her toilet training. But the point is, it was left to her own timing.

Although these examples make it sound awfully easy, you can also expect "tough" situations.

My son, age three, watched during the day as his nine-month-old little sister was the center of attention with her newfound abilities to wave bye-bye and clap. Although toilet trained, he went behind the draperies at the end of the day and pooped in his pants, as if to say "See what I can do."

34. Parent
Support Groups

PARENTS MAY NEED OTHERS with whom they can commiserate on the fears and share the joys and hopes, the ups and downs of parenthood and infancy. That is one reason I suggest that parents give themselves plenty of opportunities to get together with other parents.

Not only does it feel comforting to know that you are not alone, but parents can help each other in many practical ways, beyond sharing ideas and information. Parents need to have some time away from their infants, but with the reassurance that their children are well cared-for.

A regularly scheduled small group allows parents to observe the behavior and development of infants and also to observe other parents with their babies. Seeing the differences and similarities in personalities and parenting styles can give a broader perspective to one's own parenting.

Children, too, will look forward to regularly repeated meetings with the same children. They learn to interact with other infants and to accept and trust a few other carers besides their own parents. Slowly this prepares them to grow into the wider world of child care, preschool, etc.

It takes time, effort, and dedication to initiate and carry through such a program: to find parents who are compatible, with children of similar age range; to collect appropriate play equipment; to choose and childproof a space (it gives the infants more predictability to meet at the same location and to find objects in the same place each time); to decide how often and how many hours per week the group should meet (possibly two hours per week for infants, increasing slowly up to three or more for toddlers). Participating parents could alternate responsibility for being in charge of the group (while the others stay to observe, help, or eventually leave) and could also meet in the evening without the children to evaluate and discuss the program.

With regular attendance and participation, there is no end to the benefits a well-organized support group can provide.

35. Decisions, Decisions (on Working)

M ANY MOTHERS AND FATHERS work full-time after their babies are born and feel they must, for economic or psychological or many other reasons. Quite often when people say "I have to...," however, it really means "I *want* to...." It is not always easy to take a stand and do what you really want to do— and then admit it.

Parents who enjoy their outside jobs may come home much more refreshed, more ready for being with their child. Parents need self-time, just as a child needs self-time.

Parents who choose to be at home full-time *also* need time away from their children. Even if it is a single, quiet, private hour a day, a parent must not stifle his or her individuality for the children. But I also do not want these same parents to feel that they *must* get out, must work, must do something else other than what many of them really want to do the most: that is, staying home and parenting full-time. I still recommend, if it is economically feasible, for at least one of the parents to wait those first few years before going out into the world on a full-time basis. Sure, it is a sacrifice—financially, even creatively—but there is time, so much time later. You must ask yourself, "What would really happen if I *didn't* work right now...? or if I worked fewer hours...?"

Please consider that never in his or her life will your child develop and change so rapidly—every day can bring a new little miracle. If at all possible, do not miss it! And if you want to work, try to find part-time work. Although a whole day with a baby may seem long sometimes, in retrospect parents often feel that the first two or so years "just flew away."

The RIE approach can help avoid some of the frustrations of the "ongoingness" of parenting by structuring life so that both you and your baby can enjoy times of togetherness as well as separateness while your baby independently explores her environment. You do not need to become a slave to your child. Then by the time the child learns to communicate with language, she will be more ready to tolerate other caregivers in your absence if you choose later to return to other gratifying work of your own.

36. Infant Care Alternatives

SINGLE PARENTS, AND PARENTS who are both working, must ask themselves what sort of care situation would be satisfying to both them and their infant. Parents who know that they have provided the best, most loving solution will feel positive about their choice. I believe that, if you want something strongly enough, you will find it.

One Caregiver

I would like for those parents who cannot be with their child to find one caregiver with whom they feel confident and comfortable and pay that person to take care of their child. Hopefully, this helper would feel a commitment and take great interest in the job, since it would involve the most important profession that exists. The helper's ongoing sensitive responses to the infant's small signals build mutual trust and confidence.

Child Care Centers

Some child care centers are very good, but few are very good for children under two years of age. Though state and federal regulations have been established, even when met, they do not currently insure that the needs of infants are met, too.

In my consulting work with a great variety of centers, I have found that, while the people in charge are usually well-meaning, child-loving people wanting to do a decent job, this rarely is possible for many reasons.

Even nationwide, too few centers have a consistent philosophy and methodology to serve as good models for other infant care centers; and comprehensive ongoing staff training is not widely available.[5] Most often, salaries and morale are low, with high staff turnover rates. Infants must constantly adjust to changing people and their different approaches. Spaces are often inadequate (rooms too large, or too small, without direct access to safe outdoor areas; not enough natural light).

It is almost impossible to give infants a peaceful environment because too many people are coming and going, there is too much noise, there is too much artificial light, there is too much everything.

Toward Another Solution

Some parents consider taking their child with them to work; and the idea of accomplishing paid, productive work while providing tender, loving care is enticing. Yet the reality is that few, if any, work places have the appropriate environments for growing infants and even fewer for toddlers. In my mind this is a typical neither-nor situation: the parent can pay full attention neither to her child nor to her work. As a result, the child, the parent, and the employer all are shortchanged.

What may be a better solution is some type of on-site care facility in which parents could spend a certain amount of time

---

[5]   Since this was written, RIE has become actively involved in improving infant care in groups by offering professional training as well as an accreditation process and consultation for centers. (See, *About RIE*, page 191, and an example of the application of the approach in a RIE center, page 193–201, and a family day care home, page 203–211.)

feeding, caring for and just being with their infants at different times during their working day. Each room would be set up for a few infants (not more than four) with a well-trained infant caregiver. This would have many of the benefits of a child care center without some of the typical drawbacks (e.g., having too many infants in a group and having infants separated from their parents for long hours at a time). It could be within or not far from the work place. It could follow RIE's recommendation for creating safe environments with minimal furniture, such as cribs and a diapering table; and simple play materials, such as un-breakable containers, bowls, crates, and balls. Parents could collect the equipment; or it could be more extensively supported by the employer, such as covering overhead expenses and the salary of each infant care worker.

Knowing that their children are in a child-oriented environment with a reliable person, and being able to visit their children several times a day, gives parents peace of mind. Rather than feeling guilty for not being with their children, or guilty for not concentrating fully on their work, parents with such an arrangement may produce even better work and derive more satisfaction from it.

Evaluating a Care Situation for Your Infant

What should parents look for or demand of a good care situation? One approach is to ask yourself: *If I were the infant, would I like to be here?*

- Does the environment allow me to be able to do everything that I naturally would do?
- Are there opportunities for me to anticipate what will happen next?

- Is there a large enough and absolutely safe space in which I can move freely?
- Is there a selection of safe and appropriate objects from which I can choose?
- Am I given time to play without interruption?
- Can I do what is expected of me?
- If I cry, do I know the person[6] who will respond?
- If I am tired, do I have a peaceful place to sleep?
- Does my caregiver observe closely in order to understand my needs?
- Am I given time to work out my own conflicts as much as possible?
- Does my caregiver give me full attention while caring for me?
- Will my caregiver stay with me when I am a toddler?
- Are my parents welcome to visit me at any time?

---

[6] Since the time of my work with Dr. Pikler in the 1940's, I have believed that an infant needs an intimate, stable relationship with few people. If infants must be in group care, I advocate having a small group of infants with one primary ongoing caregiver.

37. Fads and Trends in Child Rearing (What Is the Rush?)

EVER SINCE THE EXISTENCE of humans we have been raising children. Are we getting any better at it? Thousands of books have been written. Have they helped? More and more "experts" teach a garden variety of methods. Do they work? I sometimes wonder whether this overload of information does not create more confusion than understanding.

The pendulum of child-rearing practices swings back and forth. Fads come and go quickly. We must be persistent if we want to help parents see the difference between what is universal and what is a changing fad in child rearing, so that more infants may grow up into authentic children and adults.

We should not be too gullible about anything "new." On the contrary, we should evaluate every "new and improved" theory and gimmick using logical reasoning. You always have a few people who have crazy ideas.

Infant "Stimulation"

Stimulation to me means interruption. I believe what infants *are* doing is very important, and we should try to schedule daily life so there are hardly any interruptions in the daily routine of sleeping, eating and free exploration. What upsets me the most are the many messages parents get that young infants *need* more stimulation—e.g., that a six-month-old benefits from shopping at a supermarket, or a nine-month-old learns from watching children's television, or a 10-month-old *wants* to go to activity classes.

What a sad and unsuccessful "make believe" parents develop—they learn to expect and see what they want to see, rather than the reality. Why do parents not relax, observe, and enjoy what their infant is capable of doing; why do so many choose to worry and work hard to try to *make* them do what they are not capable of?

Too Much, Too Early

Many parents, teachers, physicians and other professionals spend time and energy trying to speed up development, to force children to do what they cannot do, or to teach what they are not yet capable of. How sad. Nobody gains except the many who take money by manufacturing gadgets which supposedly speed up the natural developmental process.

While some people may respond to the voice of reason and begin to question what is really best for their infants, I fear many more will be lured by multi-colored parachutes and flash cards of painters and brain parts. As a result, more and more babies will be tossed up in the air, taught irrelevant information, treated like objects, and fed data like computers. It is like force feeding the child with food he or she cannot digest.

Parents may try so hard to "teach" their children that they do not realize just what the children are learning from them. When infants do not understand what is being asked of them, all they learn is to respond to their parents' cues, however unintentional they may be—facial expression, tone of voice, subtle gestures. Infants learn to perform, like elephants in the circus—not appreciated for just being themselves, but for doing tricks.

Why is it so difficult to accept the importance of readiness? Normally developing young children *do* what they can do; they do not withhold. Parents who expect their children to perform on a level the child has not yet reached are creating failure and disappointment for both their children and themselves.

Don't people realize how it possibly affects young infants, when what they *can* do is not appreciated but what they *cannot* do is expected? What a sad and confusing experience it must be to grow up never living up to your parents' expectations. And how frustrating it must be for parents not to be able to enjoy what their child is actually doing. It seems to me everybody is losing.

Wouldn't life be easier for both parents and infants if parents would observe, relax and enjoy what their young child *is* doing, rather than keep teaching what the child is not yet capable of?

Parents may not realize the high price they may have to pay for their ambitious endeavors to speed up infancy and interfere with natural growth. They may never connect early stressful training with problems frequently encountered later on: from sleeping and eating disorders to nervous and self-destructive behaviors (hair-pulling, nail-biting, stuttering, nervous tics, or anorexia); from disinterested, bored and unmotivated students to early school dropouts and drug abusers. While the effect of any environment is dependent on the child's personality, vulnerability and resilience, some of these children may need intensive psychotherapy at some point. But I have yet to hear of a single case in which a person (coming from loving parents and an average, responsive environment) sought therapy because he or she had not been *taught* enough during infancy.

If we think of the fact that a healthy, normal child learns to walk, to talk, to understand and communicate in three years, we could truly call these the miraculous years. The rest of the time, children expand on this basic knowledge. Why would anybody try to interfere with this perfect early development?

What Is the Rush?

Infants throughout the centuries have always been the most powerless of humans and have been forced to accept roles imposed upon them. Our "instant" society likes to produce "instant" know-it-alls. Parents compete with each other over whose child achieves first and faster... reading, numbers, acrobatics, etc.

Unfortunately, the tendency of our time for the last decades has changed from the concept of readiness to "the earlier, the better." Too many "experts" put pressure on parents to try to teach their infants earlier and earlier.

What is the rush? Isn't the life span getting longer and longer? Don't we have more time than ever to learn leisurely, being guided by our own interest and readiness?

Time and time again I have asked parents, "How old were you when you learned to sit?" So far nobody could remember. What is the benefit of early sitting? Why are so many people hooked on concepts such as "sooner is better"? Since our life span is getting longer—why not slow down? Why are concepts such as readiness and motivation hardly mentioned?

Why is earlier better? Why spend money and energy in wanting to do the impossible? Who gains? Well, all the people and organizations who make money by selling gadgets, equipment, "educational" toys, books, classes, etc. to insecure, anxious parents.

Infants do not need anxious parents *or* gadgets. They need time, time to develop according to their inner biological schedule.

You know, we live in a very speeded-up society. You have to

154

do this, you have to get here, you have to drive there, there's always rush, rush, rush and have to, have to. And many times what we do takes more time, more energy, more money, more everything, so it does not make it easier. What price do our children pay for our doing to them so many things that they really do not need? Why do we do it?

I have spent my adult life trying to figure out why parents and society put themselves into a race—what is the hurry? I keep trying to convey the pleasure every parent and teacher could feel while observing, appreciating and enjoying what the infant is doing. This attitude would change our educational climate from worry to joy. Can anybody argue about the benefits for a child who is appreciated and enjoyed for what she can do and does naturally? Try to realize how confusing it must feel to a young infant who is pulled up into a sitting position, propped with pillows and thus made immobile and insecure. Too early, too much, too fast means developmentally inappropriate.

If we could observe and see infants as completely competent for the stage at which they are, we would learn from and about them rather than teach them. Being around infants should remind us how to be "real," "genuine," "authentic."

What infants need is the opportunity and *time* to take in and figure out the world around them.

I believe this issue is so basic, so important, that it cannot be overstated.

38. Absolutely Safe!

ONE THING THAT IS A BATTLE for me in the United States, and I cannot say I am winning it, is to have a physically safe environment for infants and children.

At different cities throughout my travels, I feel encouraged and pleased when I learn how many people know about RIE. And it is interesting for me to sort out what information our RIE parents accept more easily than others. I continue to be surprised that a very important part of our teaching is neither heard, understood nor followed. It is *safety*.

I consider safety the prerequisite for implementing the RIE approach. By safety I mean an environment which is so totally safe that, even *without* any adult supervision, the infant or toddler would be totally safe.

Why is it so difficult for parents to create such a safe place?

Parents sometimes casually tell me that they never leave the baby alone: "Well, I do not have a totally safe place for the baby to leave him alone." To my question, "Not even to go to the bathroom?" they reply, "I do take him with me" or "While I take a shower I put her in a walker or swing to keep her out of trouble." This is doubly stressful: the child is left by the parent *and* prevented from moving freely and safely. Why is it so difficult to convince parents that a safe room with gates at all doors not only frees the infant but the parent as well?

Whenever I am invited to a place where there is a child, I almost always find something that is physically unsafe. And I almost always get the same answer when I ask questions: "Nothing has ever happened." And I say, "Something could happen in another five minutes or perhaps tomorrow." When I visit infant care facilities and find something unsafe, the people in charge say, "The children never go there." My answer is always, "Not yet."

No matter how often I hear it, it still scares me when people reassure me that they never leave children unattended. This, of course, is not possible.

Having a totally safe place is a *must*. It is a foundation on which the rest of the RIE approach is built.

39. Equipment: What Is Really Necessary?

SOMETIMES, WITHOUT REALIZING, parents interfere with an infant's mobility or problem-solving ability by using equipment which some people think babies need.

At RIE we try to give parents strength not to fall victim to the incredible bombardment of sales pitches, free gifts, brochures, etc., for all those wonderful-sounding gadgets that are touted as keeping your baby happy and content while stimulating her and accelerating her intelligence.

Recommendations

In order for infants and parents to live peacefully together, no special products are needed except for one: gates for all the doors to the infant room. I encourage even expectant parents to think of gates! (See, *Time Apart: A Space for Your Baby*, page 15)

In starting out with your baby, there are, of course, other items you will find helpful. Buy a bassinet or small crib, a diapering table, a chest of drawers, a small bathtub and an approved car safety seat. (For newborns up to 17 pounds, there is one bassinet-type car seat in which the infant can lie flat, which many of our RIE parents and I prefer.)

Simple objects that infants can manipulate in many ways, not needing adult help or supervision, are the best toys and learning tools (See, *Choosing Play Objects*, page 97). A duplicate crib and playpen for outdoors are excellent investments. (See, *Outdoor*

Living, page 103) We also recommend a low chair and table for eating when your toddler can sit up on his own. (See, *Feeding*, page 83)

What Not to Buy

What you do *not* need are bouncers, swings, walkers, high chairs and other *restrictive devices*.

At RIE we believe that the infant should be able to move and explore freely, to choose and change his own body position, to come and go as he wants—within the safe and challenging environment we create. We recommend that you do not put a baby into a position which he cannot get into by himself. (See, *At Their Own Time, and In Their Own Way*, page 53)

People have the illusion that walkers help children learn to walk. But in order to walk, you have to do two things: one, you have to be able to support your weight, which you do not do in a walker; and two, you have to learn to balance on one foot. And if you cannot do these, then you cannot walk.

A walker is like a moving prison that prevents babies from doing what they would naturally be doing. Everything they do naturally while moving on the floor prepares them to walk. Babies need to go through many stages before they walk; they do not need to be taught. Infants who have learned each stage of the process of walking naturally do not hurt themselves badly when they fall.

Some people say they put babies in walkers so they will be "safe," but babies can get into accidents in walkers. Some people put babies in walkers or swings so the babies will be "happy," but instead the babies just "tune out," and this "solution" is only easier for the adults because the babies do not cry.

I would also discourage you from propping your baby in an

infant seat, except if you need to put the baby into the shopping cart in the supermarket. (A better solution, however, is not to take the baby with you.)

If you have to go somewhere, baby carriers are preferable to strollers which do not support infants' backs. Use them for your convenience and for as short a time as possible. (See, *Holding,* page 45)

Infants also do *not* need those *"new and better" toys* for which there are so many commercial pressures. Expensive, complex toys designed to be used certain ways rarely give children opportunities to explore and use them in their own way. Toys designed to entertain create passive onlookers, future television addicts, rather than curious, actively learning children. Think of the children who are lost and bored unless entertained and who keep asking, "What shall I do now?"

Rattles are an adult idea: you pick up something, and it makes noise. Why does it make noise? Because some adult put something into something. Mobiles are intrusive—the infant has no choice. Who chose the mobile? An adult.

Infants do not need additional visual stimulation and entertainment at an age when they are newly out of the womb and already exposed to a bombardment of stimulation. It can take them months to figure out the crib, how you can poke a finger out here and not there. The world is full of things for babies to figure out. We interfere with their learning experiences by providing artificial things.

The idea of daily walks appealed to us, and we purchased an English perambulator (buggy). Though it was one of our more expensive investments, it has served us well in all types of weather

for nearly two years. I felt it was the most comfortable way for a young infant to travel, as she could be asleep or awake, stretch out, and seek shelter from the elements. The pram allowed Erin to be nearer the adult level [than in an "umbrella" stroller] and facing me so that we could converse with one another. This pram also came with a fold-up back rest, useful when Erin was at the sitting-up stage, with a belt around her middle to prevent her from falling out. We used the pram nearly every day for the first eighteen months and a few more times until nearly age two, when Erin enjoyed being more independent on our walks.

40. Wishes for the Future

I HAVE A VISION of a "gentler, kinder" world and believe that there are always "islands" of peace, empathy and gentleness even in our increasingly frantic environment. I want to share with you my special wishes for the future.

Wishes for Infants and Toddlers

I wish children could grow according to their natural pace: sleep when sleepy, wake up when rested, eat when hungry, cry when upset, express feelings, play and explore without being unnecessarily interrupted; in other words, be allowed to grow and blossom as each was meant to.

I wish infants would not have to perform for their parents, not be sat up when only ready for rolling, not be assisted to walk when only ready for crawling. A child can be pushed to do these things but physiologically may not be really ready. In our culture we push to attain these states faster than they are naturally reached.

I wish children would not have to reassure parents of their effectiveness, i.e., smile when frustrated, clap hands when sleepy. I wish children did not have to cope with a parental attitude that says, "If my child smiles at me, this shows I am a good parent."

I wish children did not have to be ping-pong balls between parents. I wish children did not have to be experimental subjects for toy manufacturers, cereal makers, new fads or theories in child care.

Wishes for Parents

I wish parents would feel secure, but not rigid. I wish they would be accepting, but set limits; be available, but not intruding.

I wish parents would be patient, but "true to thine own self." I wish parents could arrive at a balance between giving quality time to their children and to themselves. I wish parents could achieve a state of self-respect and give equal respect to their children. I wish parents could resist new fads and the many pressures to buy elaborate and expensive products which babies do not need.

I wish we could eliminate old assumptions about fatherhood, i.e., that being warm and gentle is not "manly" or that fathers are expected to be tough—to throw infants into the air, or blow cigarette smoke in their faces (yes, I have seen this done "playfully"). Rough-housing not only scares babies, it may even cause brain damage. Playful activities should not be forced by the parent. I would like fathers not to be afraid to be themselves, to know that they can be tender and soothing and quiet and still be "manly."

How I welcome the realization among more and more fathers that the human relationship with their infants can be gratifying and rewarding.

Wishes for Families

I wish doctors had enough time to be able to observe how a baby is moving naturally, to share these observations with parents, and to point out to the parents how competent the baby is at any stage of development. This might help the parents to observe and appreciate what the child is capable of doing and to stop worrying and pushing toward the next milestone, for which the baby may not yet be ready.

I wish caregivers could be fully observant and really know what goes on with infants: how they react, when to intervene and when *not* to intervene.

We need to make the care of infants and toddlers as consistent as it can be, with as much continuity of caregivers as possible. I wish babies and their parents did not have to be separated so much. Infants always need to believe that they are loved because of who they are. We need sensitive caregivers who can communicate that.

I would like the people who work with infants to be appreciated and well paid—not overpaid, because it should not be done by people who do it for the money. Educaring should be done by very capable people who also make a decent living.

And do you know what I wish above all else? That we each don't lose sight of laughter—that through all of the pain we might see and feel around us, we maintain our sense of humor. People who take life too seriously are terrible to live with!

41. On Loving

FOR YEARS AND YEARS when talking to groups of parents, I asked them, "What do infants need beyond food, rest, warmth, hygiene, etc.?" The answer was unanimously, "Love." But what is love?

Rather than trying to explain or analyze "love" theoretically, I will share with you from my own experiences how it feels to be loved and how it feels to love. It makes me feel good, it opens me up, it gives me strength. I feel less vulnerable, lonely, helpless, confused. I feel more honest, more rich. It fills me with hope, trust, creative energy. It refuels me and prepares me to face life.

How do I perceive the other person who gives me these feelings? I see him or her as honest, as one who sees and accepts me for what I really am, who responds to me objectively without being too critical. I respect his authenticity and values and he respects mine. He is one who is available when needed, who listens and hears, who looks and sees me, who genuinely shares himself. In short, I perceive one who loves me, who gives me these feelings, as one who cares.

In no other loving connection is "caring" as crucial as in the parent/infant relationship. This relationship is, at first, one-sided. It is the parent who is the giver; the child slowly learns to give.

There are many definitions of love. I recommend that parents read *The Art of Loving* by Eric Fromm, who defines love as caring, respecting, assuming responsibility for and acquiring knowledge about the other person. If love is defined in this way, harmful acts are not attributed to "love." (In Shakespeare's "Othello,"

Desdemona is killed by her husband, with the thought, "I kill you and keep loving you." Is this true love?)

Demonstrating Love

To care is to put love into action. The way we care for our babies is then how they experience our love.

How and when do you pick up your baby? For instance, when you are in a hurry, do you pick him up without warning or plop him down abruptly? Are you responding to the baby's needs or to your own?

When do you smile at your baby? If your infant could express the bewilderment she feels when looking at her mother's smiling face while being propped in an uncomfortable position, it might sound like, "Mommy, why do you smile at me when I feel so uncomfortable?"

How do you talk to your infant? Do you tell him "I love you" just when you are at the end of your tolerance, when what you really feel is "I wish I never had a baby"? When what you say is inconsistent with what you feel, your baby receives a double message. Rather than feeling reassured of your love, instead he feels confused.

When do you choose to hug and kiss your infant? Is it when you come home from a party and look at your peacefully sleeping child that you start touching and kissing her and wake her up? Although an "act of love," this was serving your needs, not the baby's.

Do you tolerate your child's crying? It seems so much easier to *do* something about crying: to pick up, move around, take for a ride, pat, bounce. When the baby cries, the first step should be to try to determine *why* he cries, rather than to try to *stop* the crying. When you have eliminated hunger and the other standard

168

discomforts and the baby is still crying, that is the time to tolerate crying, even to respect the infant's right to cry. You might want to say, "I am here to help you, but I do not know what you need. Try to tell me." If that is what you feel, share it; this is the beginning of communication.

How do you set limits and restrain your infant or toddler? Some parents are afraid that setting limits or disagreeing with a child will be perceived as unloving. Yet sometimes setting a limit is in the best interest of the infant or toddler and is therefore an act of love. Even though the child may be protesting, you know that what you are doing is for the child's sake. The most obvious example is the baby's car seat: even when she objects to being strapped into it, you continue with the task because you know that it keeps her safe.

Do you allow your baby to experience some frustration? It is difficult for parents to learn that they cannot spare their children from all pain and frustration. Yet the best way anybody can develop tolerance for frustration is by experiencing and directly dealing with it in small, manageable amounts.

In what ways do you allow your infant to explore freely and to make choices? Some ways of showing love may prevent an infant from making choices or engaging in exploration. For instance, do you hold your baby in your lap in such a way that he can leave when he indicates he is ready, or do you hold on to him? Holding a child may keep the child back from free exploration, making him passive and overly dependent. Showing love means being available, rather than intrusive.

Do you tell your child how you really feel? How confusing for a child to have a parent who pretends to be the always-loving, always-cheerful person. If you learn to communicate how you are feeling (tired, peaceful, upset, joyful, angry, etc.), you become authentic and allow your child to grow up authentic.

Dear parent, we all agree that babies need love. Most people associate parental love with the easy solutions of holding, nursing, cuddling. What is much more difficult is to find the balance between holding on and letting go. It is a lifelong struggle, and maybe the hardest part of parenting.

42. Does RIE Make a Difference?

*R*AISING A CHILD *using the RIE approach has been a happy, fulfilling experience, but does it really make a difference? Children seem to adapt and survive their circumstances no matter how they are raised, as long as it is with love. In a playground full of children, can I tell which ones are "RIE babies" and which are not? Given all our differences in development and personality, it is hard to attribute everything to RIE, but I have some observations about it and my experience.*

In the realm of parenting, using RIE is a much calmer and gentler way to raise a child. After attending RIE classes for a year and a half, I find that I don't have many struggles with my son because our world is not set up for conflict.

One RIE tenet says, "Do less—enjoy more." I try to keep that in mind. I can let my child do his own exploring and develop at his own pace. I don't need to teach him everything, stimulate him at each stage of development, or assume that I always know the best and the right way to do things. I try to let him solve his own problems and to provide an environment in which he can experiment, discover and create.

He has learned to engage himself in his own activities rather than to depend on someone or something else. He is able to play alone, or with friends, for long periods of time. At mealtimes, I sit with him as he sits at his own small table and feeds himself. He shows little interest in TV or videotapes and other activities where he is a passive participant; he prefers to be active. He has exquisite posture and a graceful athleticism which I attribute to the RIE approach.

I work to make a calm home where he feels safe and supported. I am delighted by the intimate interaction we have during practical routines of daily life. In addition, I am very grateful to have one uniting, centering philosophy with my husband. We have a philosophy and a strategy which has worked so far.

And no, I cannot always find the RIE parent, but he or she is usually the one at the playground who isn't interfering with her child's play, who seems relaxed and less stressed, the one who offers a warning before it's time to leave, and the one whose children help pick up the toys and leave without making a fuss.

43. One Family, One Saturday

ONE SATURDAY WE expected friends for dinner. Our car needed emergency repair, the house needed cleaning, the clothes needed washing, and dinner needed to be prepared by 7:00 p.m. Our day went like this:

8:00 a.m. *Corina woke up, played by herself, and was cooing in her crib. We could hear her tossing and turning over. Our alarm had not gone off yet.*

8:30 a.m. *We got up. Corina heard this and started making louder sounds. I greeted her and asked her if she wanted to be picked up. She reached toward me with her arms and legs. I picked her up; and she started sucking my shoulder, indicating she was hungry. I fed her, being fully attentive to her while doing it.*

9:10 a.m. *Corina's diaper needed changing, so we proceeded into our cooperative venture together. "Corina, we need to change your diaper. Are you ready?" She responded by waving her arms and legs toward me. I then picked her up and told her, "I'll put you down on the table." "Your wet diaper is coming off," I told her, while I took off the diaper. She looked and waited. "I'll put your dry diaper on. Could you put your legs down?" She put her legs down, several seconds later. "Now we are done. I will take you down."*

9:15 a.m. *I sat on the floor in her room with her and watched her play. She would glance at me every now and then. About ten minutes later, I told her that I would be in the kitchen having* *breakfast with Papa. We had breakfast, then I proceeded to sort the laundry in the kitchen, while her father began to fix the car, after telling Corina that he would be outside for a while.*

9:45 a.m. *I heard some complaining sounds. "Corina, I heard you. What do you want?" I got down on the floor and smelled she needed diaper changing. "Oh, it seems that you're telling me you want to be changed. I'll pick you up now." I changed her, without hurrying. As I left her room, I told her that I would do the laundry and I would be in the kitchen.*

10:15 a.m. *I loaded the clothes into the washer and vacuumed the living room. About half an hour later, I heard some complaining sounds from Corina. As I listened, the sounds evolved from complaining to contented, and I resumed my work.*

10:55 a.m. *As I passed Corina's room, I saw her in a sitting position; and her balance was very shaky and tenuous. I said to her, "Oh, it looks as if you are stuck and cannot move yourself. I will give you some help." I lifted her bottom and waited for her to pull her legs out. "There, you got yourself unstuck." She still was fussing, so I asked her if she wanted to be picked up. She moved a little in my direction and I picked her up. We sat on the floor for several minutes; then she wiggled, wanting to get down. She crawled across the room, picked up her shiny bowl, and grabbed the measuring spoons. In a few minutes, I told her I would be in the kitchen to finish the laundry.*

11:15 a.m. *Just finished the vacuuming when the dryer went off. Shortly afterward, Corina started to complain, so I brought the clothes to be folded where she could see me. As I folded the clothes, I showed her what each item was and told her to whom it belonged. I folded the entire load; and as I was folding the last piece, she wanted to be picked up. "Corina, I will finish this and then I'll pick you up right away," I told her. She responded by waiting quietly.*

I kept my end of the bargain and devoted my full attention to her while I fed her.

12 noon–2:30 p.m. *Corina took a nap.*

2:35 p.m. *She woke up and snuggled on my shoulder for a while. A few minutes later, she was wiggly and wanted to be put down. I laid her on her back, and she immediately turned over and grabbed the toy car. She then held her scarf. I left a few minutes later, after telling her that I would be cooking in the kitchen.*

3:00 p.m. *She started to cry, so I stayed with her in her room. She played and looked at me. Several minutes later, she started to cry again. I checked her clothes and diapers but saw that she did not need changing. I realized that she was hungry when she started crying loudly even while being held. I told her, "Oh, now I realize what you want. I'll feed you right away." After she was fed, we went outside to the front lawn.*

3:30 p.m. *I laid her down on the mat. She first looked at the leaves, the trees, listened to the birds and then turned over as a car passed by. Corina then decided to be adventurous and got off the mat into the grass. She touched it for a long while. As she was crawling, she got stuck on the lower portion of the lawn. She cried. I got down on the grass with her. "Corina, you got stuck. I know it's difficult to go uphill from where you are." She looked at me, still complaining. "Do you need help?" I asked. She did not respond but tried to move herself up the slope. When she finally got up, she smiled. We both smiled as she struggled on her own to master that new task.*

4:30 p.m. *Her father took over for me while I started dinner. Corina played in the living room while he read magazines. When she started to complain, he unhurriedly went to her and asked her what she wanted. When he picked her up, I could hear him say, "Oh, you wanted some attention, huh?"*

What could have been an unpleasant and hectic day was actually relaxed and productive. Through our interactions with her, we give Corina quality time; through her sense of competence and confidence, she provides us with our own quality time.

44. Appreciating RIE

*D*ISCOVERING RIE IS *one of the few things that I can honestly say changed my life.*

I came to RIE a sleep-deprived, nervous, over-concerned mother of a nine-month-old. I was trying so hard to do everything right, even perfectly, that I had no idea how to get to know my own child, what he really needed and how I might begin to provide it for him. In my effort to be a perfect mother, I was failing miserably and feeling more desperate and inadequate every day.

Talking to other mothers didn't help much. Most weren't doing much better than I, which was consoling but didn't help me find any clues as to what I was doing wrong. I read books, I watched child-care "experts" on TV, I studied the few mothers I knew—usually those on their second child, who seemed somewhat more in control, certainly less frantic than I. Asking lots of questions, I tried in vain to find out what it was that they knew and I didn't. I'd hear general things like, "Follow your instincts." Well, fine, that's what I was doing; and it was getting me nowhere. "You have to have a schedule." Great, now how do I tell him that? Or, "Let him cry it out." I tried that…. After seventy minutes of screaming, I gave up.

Then I found RIE and Magda. The first day I visited, I found a calmness and a sense of purpose that made me feel, "This place is different." There is no short list of helpful hints, a quick fix, an easy answer. That was a relief. I kept feeling so inadequate whenever someone's capsule of advice had no effect. They made it sound so simple and easy that the problem must have been me or my baby;

we just couldn't do it.

Magda's philosophy slowly began to reveal itself to me. Subtle changes began to take place in how I was relating to my baby. I was able to get Max on something like a schedule for part of the day, and he started sleeping through the night.

No, actually it wasn't him—it was me. I learned that it was my responsibility to commit to a regular meal time and bath time; it was not up to Max. I had been afraid of making a rule, thinking it was up to him to decide when he would want to eat. I now understood that it was up to me to set an appropriate time for a meal and provide food; it would then be Max's choice to eat it or not. I began to see Max's crying as his rightful expression of discomfort or anger and not a criticism of my mothering. I did not have to be, nor should I be, responsible for making everything okay for him every moment. I could allow him to be angry and support him in finding his own way to cope, without feeling like I was somehow failing as a mother. I began to feel something I had not felt before: that I did know how to care for my baby. By doing less, I began to feel as if I was actually competent as a mother. I began to have an understanding of what respecting the baby meant. It did not mean catering to him or abdicating responsibility for his care; it meant providing, allowing him to have a say and learning to listen to his way of communicating his say.

Magda and RIE have made me realize that any *moment with my child is important, not just the so-called significant moments. Yes, the first step is a thrilling moment, but how much more so if we have learned to appreciate all the intricacies that are constantly changing which make that step happen.*

Now as the pretty well organized, almost rested, occasionally even relaxed mother of Max, three and a half, and Molly, two, I look back on the confused and frantic mother I was when I came to RIE three years ago; and I am so grateful to Magda and the RIE philosophy for giving me the ability to enjoy my children and my life. I have gained so much confidence and knowledge, and I know my children will reap the benefits for their lifetimes.

Thank you, Magda. From all of us.

45. Educaring – Some Examples

I N ORDER TO HIGHLIGHT the difference between other caregivers and trained Educarers, whether in the home or in other care situations, here are some illustrations:

Infants' Abilities
- Whereas many caregivers rely on infant curricula, books, and packaged programs as prescriptions to teach, drill, and speed up new skills in the areas of gross motor, social/emotional or language development, *Educarers trust the infants' abilities* to initiate their own activities, choose from available objects and work on their own projects without interruption.

Free Movement and Exploration
- Whereas others may place very young babies on their stomachs, *Educarers place very young babies on their backs*, where they can see and hear better, breathe with more ease, and be in the place of most mobility and most stability.
- Whereas others teach and encourage postures and means of locomotion which the infants are not yet able to do on their own, thus hampering free movement and exploration and sometimes even creating bodily discomfort, *Educarers provide appropriate space* for

infants to initiate their own movements freely, without interference, thus helping them to feel comfortable, competent, and self-reliant.

Sensitive Observation

- Whereas others focus on eliciting responses to their stimulation, *Educarers focus upon observing the whole child*, his or her reaction to the caregiving person, to the environment, and to peers, thus learning about the infant's personality and needs. Infants find stimulation everywhere.

Anticipation

- Whereas others may swoop up an infant unexpectedly from behind, thereby startling and interrupting the infant, and creating resistance, *Educarers always tell the infant before they do anything with the infant*, thus more often getting cooperation.

Encouraging Independence

- Whereas others select and put objects/toys in the infant's hands, *Educarers place the objects/toys so that the infant must make an effort* to reach and grasp. The child works towards what she wants.
- Whereas others encourage dependency by assuming an active role, such as by "rescuing" crying infants immediately or solving their problems for them, *Educarers wait a while* to see if the infants are capable of consoling themselves and finding their own solutions, thus encouraging autonomy.

Authenticity

- Whereas others may often use bottles and/or pacifiers to soothe a crying child, creating a false oral need for food and sucking, *Educarers accept a child's right to show both positive and negative feelings.* Educarers do not try to stop the crying, but rather they try to understand and attend to the child's real needs, such as sleepiness, hunger, or cold. If the infant soothes himself by thumb-sucking, Educarers accept this as a positive self-comforting activity.

Infant-Infant Interactions

- Whereas others often restrict infant-infant interaction (such as infants touching each other) for fear of their hurting one another, *Educarers facilitate interactions by closely observing* in order to know when to intervene and when not to.

- Whereas, in a situation of conflict between infants, others resolve the problem by separating, distracting, or deciding who should have the toy or object in question, *Educarers offer impartial comments* such as, "Both you, John, and you, Anne, want that toy." Often after such comments, minor conflicts resolve themselves.

- Whereas others may become aggressive in controlling an "aggressor," thereby reinforcing the aggressive behavior, *Educarers model appropriate behavior* by touching the aggressive child and quietly saying something like, "Easy, gently... nice."

- Whereas others may rush to pick up, to rescue, and to console the "victim" of the "aggressor," Educarers squat down, touch, and stroke the "victim," saying something like, "Gently, now, nice." By concurrently stroking and talking to both the "victim" and the "aggressor," *Educarers* model and *console both children* without reinforcing a pattern of becoming a "victim."

Individualized Caregiving

- Whereas others like to have more people or helpers in the room, *Educarers want to become the steady person to their own small group* of about four infants.
- Whereas others may become exhausted from picking up one child and putting down another, as if extinguishing one fire after another, *Educarers calmly observe* and can often prevent the "fire."

All of these examples illustrate that, while both these other caregivers and Educarers love the infant, *Educarers demonstrate love by showing and teaching respect.*

46. Reflections on My Work with Dr. Pikler

"**I**F ONLY A FEW INFANTS will benefit from this book, it was worth writing it." Although these words clearly reflect my own sentiment with this book, *Dear Parent*, they were written by Dr. Emmi Pikler in her first book for parents (1946).

Many of the ideas we teach at RIE are based on Dr. Pikler's research and clinical work with infants in Budapest, Hungary. How fortunate I am to have had her as a doctor, a teacher and a friend for close to half a century.

Who was Dr. Pikler? In many countries she would not need an introduction at all. She, as well as her accomplishments, are well known.

When I met Dr. Pikler, her ideas seemed so natural, sensible and simple. It all began when she substituted for my regular pediatrician. The way she talked to and treated my four-year-old daughter was so unusual, so unusually respectful, that it made me feel that this was the answer to all my questions and doubts I'd had ever since my first child was born.

Later I had the privilege of studying and working with her, at the National Methodological Institute for Infant Care and Education (as it was then called), often referred to as "Loczy," after the street on which it is located. Since her death in 1984, it has been renamed the Emmi Pikler National Methodological Institute for

Residential Nurseries in her honor.

So profound and far-reaching was Dr. Pikler's influence upon me that I decided to make the study and care of young children my own life's work.

"Pikler Babies"

Dr. Pikler developed her unusual approach to caring for infants with her own daughter and as a private pediatrician to a few selected families in Budapest. Making weekly visits to the homes of these families, she would spend hours observing and facilitating the mutual adaptation of the infant and the family. It was said that if you went to the park and observed the children playing there, you could easily tell which ones were the "Pikler babies." They were poised and graceful, alert and friendly, and so confidently independent.

In 1946 she adapted the same philosophy to a program for orphaned children at Loczy, where she was the executive medical director. Though raised in a residential setting without their parents, the "Loczy babies" showed the same basic characteristics as the family-raised "Pikler babies."

Pikler babies are brought up under natural conditions. They each develop without interference at his or her own rate. No one worries about the date of the "milestones." No one places them in a sitting position before they are ready to sit up by themselves. No one tries to teach them to stand or walk. No rattles or other objects are put in their hand. Not even a pacifier is put in the mouth. Are they abandoned? Neglected? Ignored? By no means. Their daily lives provide plenty of natural stimulation to keep them interested. Well-selected objects are available to the infants to climb on, to look at, to touch and manipulate. And there is ample space—space in which to move freely and explore. But the infant makes the choices of how to move and how to play.

At Loczy the babies have freedom to "do their own thing" in a carefully structured environment. The "nurses" (caregivers) at Loczy were asked to make a three-year commitment and were expected to become intimately acquainted with the infants in their group. Dr. Pikler believed (and it has been reinforced by research) that infants living in an institute derive security from permanency, constancy and anticipation: time to sleep, time to eat, time to be outside, to explore inside. Within this predictable rhythm of daily life, the infants have time for uninterrupted exploratory play activities, and the carers have time to give individualized, loving attention to each of the infants during routine caregiving. Even the smallest infant is looked at, handled and talked to as an active, participating individual worthy of respect. This is unhurried quality time.

Natural Gross Motor Development

Why did Dr. Pikler choose this unusual approach when the trend was to stimulate more and teach more? It was the outcome of her studies, observations and experience.

After receiving her medical degree in Vienna while working at the famous Pirquet Clinic, she became particularly interested in the physiology of gross motor development—as it occurs in a healthy, well-cared-for infant who is neither restricted nor taught, as contrasted with the usual artificial motor development which is the result of propping, positioning and using restrictive devices (bouncer, infant seat or walkers, etc.).

Dr. Pikler postulated that, not only do these two different practices affect motor development, but they influence all other areas of growth—social, emotional, cognitive—and even character formation. She became an advocate of "non-interference"—of allowing motor development at the infant's own rate. By allowing the child freedom of movement, she suggested, parents would develop respect for their baby's individual tempo and style in other areas of development as well.

In her work with families and at Loczy, Dr. Pikler's talents as a scientific investigator and a practitioner involved in the most minute details of the everyday care of infants made her sound approach both practical and believable. Many infants reared at Loczy—often orphaned or with difficult family situations—have been studied and their growth carefully documented. One study by the World Health Organization on Loczy children in their later years shows that, unlike children raised in most institutions, they grew up into healthy, capable individuals who were able to make a good adjustment to family life.

Worldwide Influence

Dr. Pikler authored numerous articles and was the consultant on nine films made at Loczy. Her books, translated into several languages, range from popular ones for parents to textbooks for professionals and scientific monographs. She received many awards and honors, among them one for Medical Science in 1968 for her work on the physiology of gross motor development in infancy and early childhood. Yet she was most gratified by letters sent to her from all over the world from "Pikler babies," now grown up, asking her advice because they wanted to raise their infants at home in the same way they were brought up.

From Hungary to the United States

Since my days with Dr. Pikler in Hungary, I have applied her philosophy to my work with infants in the United States. Our organization in California, Resources for Infant Educarers, grew out of encouragement we received from parents and professionals who successfully used our philosophy and urged us to offer training to infant educarers. RIE-trained infant Educarers and others have taken the philosophy all over the world.

I have felt sometimes like the bridge between Dr. Pikler and American society. The lifestyle in this country makes it very difficult to raise a baby the way Emmi wanted. She had a strong feeling that if you give a young child a peaceful beginning, the child develops a natural rhythm and then later he can grow more easily into adult life. You have to respect and trust a healthy, normal baby's inborn capacities, his natural desire to learn. You do not have to do more. What infants need is the opportunity and time to take in and figure out the world around them.

What Dr. Pikler really stood for seems the simplest, the most natural thing to do. But it isn't, because our society pushes us constantly. The very essence of RIE—to create a safe, quiet environment, to slow down, pay attention, and allow the infants to move and play in their own way—is a contradiction to the prevailing attitude in our society. It is hard to understand why people resist an easier way of life that brings better results.

Dr. Pikler was a person who dared to question well-established ideologies and practices half a century ago, and I continue to do so myself. After all these years, it is touching and gratifying to see how one person's visions can endure and expand despite society's opposing trends. Why shouldn't infants get the very, very best that our society can offer?

47. About RIE

Resources for infant educarers (RIE™), founded in 1978 by Magda Gerber and Tom Forrest, M.D., is a non-profit membership organization concerned with improving the care and education of infants. RIE offers parent-infant observation and guidance classes, public workshops and conferences, training for professionals, and consultations to and accreditation of infant care centers. Other resources include books, a quarterly newsletter, audiotapes, and videos.

For those wishing to understand and use the RIE philosophy of respect in their life or work, RIE offers a basic course introducing principles and practices. The training is for directors, teachers, therapists, nurses, consultants, and all those who want to deepen their understanding of infant development, care, and education. Two advanced mentored courses—a practicum, and a three-part apprenticeship—complete the training. Certified RIE graduates, called RIE Associates, are then eligible for membership in the RIE Alliance, a professional organization for peer review and support.

For more information, contact:

Resources for Infant Educarers (RIE)
1550 Murray Circle, Los Angeles, CA 90026
(323) 663-5330, FAX (323) 663-5586
website: www.RIE.org, email: Educarer@RIE.org

By becoming a general member of RIE, you can participate in RIE's efforts to improve the quality of infant care and help enrich the lives of infants and their families in our communities.

48. A Brief Visit to a RIE Infant Center

(A Word Picture, by Ruth R. Money)

THE FIRST IMPRESSION that greets a visitor to a RIE center is one of peacefulness. The noise level is low. The infants and toddlers seem content, each one involved in his own task. The children move with grace. The center doesn't seem crowded. There are no large groups of children together. No one is rushing around. The adults are involved with the children rather than with one another. The environments in each room and outdoor space are appropriately different. As the children become older, the size of the equipment is increased to meet their developmental needs.

This center[7] cares for 12 infants and toddlers in a remodeled home divided into three classrooms: a baby room, for the youngest infants; a larger middle infant room, for the stage where they are crawling, creeping, cruising, learning to walk; and an even larger room for the toddlers. This module for 12 infants and toddlers could be replicated on a campus of two or more cottages or in a larger center, still keeping the same small, intimate atmosphere in each room.

---

[7]   The center described is the South Bay Infant Center, the first RIE demonstration center. It was founded to model the respectful caring relationships possible in a group setting where each infant is treated as an individual.

193

Infants usually enter the center when they are about three months of age and stay with the same team of two primary caregivers for two years, until they leave for preschool at about 27 months of age. One member of the caregiving team works in the morning and the other in the afternoon, as the center is open eleven hours a day. Every eight months, as a group of four toddlers "graduates," the center accepts a group of four new babies. Each team of primary caregivers moves with their infants to the next developmentally appropriate environment so that the intimate caregiving relationships are stable over the two years the infants are at the center.

First Stop – Baby Room

As we sample what is going on in different parts of this center, our first stop is a 12-foot-square room which opens through French doors to a wooden deck of about the same size. Two babies are lying on the floor very absorbed in moving their bodies in ways unique to each of them. A gate separates the play area from an area for sleeping and diaper-changing. One baby is gently cradled in a caregiver's arms as she feeds him a bottle. The fourth baby is asleep in a crib on the other side of the gate.

The caregiver is seated in a sturdy chair, devoting her complete attention to the one baby she is holding. Both adult and baby seem to be comfortable and to be enjoying the activity. As the baby sucks away, draining down the level of milk in the bottle, the adult looks into the baby's eyes, occasionally talking to him. How can the adult afford to pay so much attention to the one child she is feeding? Might the two babies on the floor get into trouble? We note that the environment in which the babies play is simple and uncluttered. A clean sheet covers a nearly room-size rug, and there are some lightweight plastic toys around, as well as a very low platform and ramp. There doesn't seem to be anything on which a baby could hurt himself or could damage.

One of the babies on the rug begins to fuss. "I hear you, Jonathan," says the adult, briefly looking at him. "I thought you would be getting hungry. I have your bottle ready to heat so I can feed you soon, but I'm feeding Ramon now." She turns her eyes back to the baby in her arms and continues to give him the bottle. "It is your time right now, Ramon," she says. Soon Ramon stops sucking. The caregiver takes the nipple out, offers it again, but Ramon spits it out. "All right," she says, "I see you are done" and puts the bottle down, then holds Ramon while she burps him. "What a good burp," she says to him and then lifts him gently and puts him on his back on the rug, where he promptly turns over onto his stomach and starts to pull himself toward a plastic colander not far away.

The educarer puts Jonathan's bottle into a crock-pot of warm water and says to him, "Your bottle will be warm in a minute, Jonathan." As she marks down the time and ounces on Ramon's feeding record, she hears Samantha making noises in her crib. The carer greets her and holds out her arms to the baby. "What a good nap you had, Samantha. I just marked it down. You slept an hour and 20 minutes. I think I had better change you before you play." Samantha holds out her arms to her carer and is picked up and carried affectionately over to the diaper table. "I'm putting you down now," she says, and lays her on her back. As Jonathan's protests grow louder, the carer continues to diaper Samantha, talking and smiling with her as she completes the tasks in a relaxed fashion. After she puts Samantha on the floor, the carer squirts the disinfectant on the diapering table, wipes it with paper towels, and washes her hands.

Then she picks up Jonathan. "Yes, you're telling me you are

very hungry. I have your bottle ready for you now," she says, as she settles him into her arms and starts the feeding process with him. She is now giving to Jonathan the same kind of comfort, attention and care that she gave to Ramon. Again the carer looks comfortable, and the baby is happily eating and looking at the adult. On the floor Ramon and Samantha are busily rolling around, but Peggy has moved to the edge of the room near a pillow and is yawning. "You look sleepy, Peggy. You have had a long play time. I'll put you in your crib in just a little while so you can sleep more comfortably," says the carer as she turns back to feeding Jonathan.

As we leave this area we realize that, except for five minutes of Jonathan's fussing, we have heard only quiet voices, and it is quiet again. Yet two babies have been fed with one-to-one attention, one baby has been picked up from a nap and her diaper has been changed in a relaxed fashion, all four babies have had a happy play time, records have been kept—and all of this with no other adult to help the caregiver.

Second Stop – Middle Infant Room

Our second stop is in the middle infant room, which has a ramp leading down to an outdoor play yard. The toy shelves on one side of the room are almost empty, and many toys are on the floor. Two children are outside with a caregiver, Ben is crawling up the ramp on all-fours to come back inside, and the fourth child is sleeping in an adjacent crib room.

Outside Gina sits in a dry turtle wading pool with numerous toys in it. She throws a few toys out, then puts her hand inside a plastic ring. Koichi is cruising around the inside edge of an elevated redwood deck, holding on to the wall. Ben, who has remained inside, climbs up and down some small wooden stairs.

The educarer watches him through the open French doors, but she does not go inside. Ben comes down from the stairs, crawls past the toys, climbs inside a shelf, and stretches out.

The carer hears a noise from the nap room. She goes inside, where Danielle is awake and standing up in her crib. All four porta-cribs in this room have had their legs adjusted so they are very close to the floor. Danielle holds out her arms, and the carer lifts her up. "I'll change your diaper at the station outside, Danielle," says the carer as she carries her outside. Danielle cooperates with the carer as her diaper is changed.

As Danielle and the caregiver are cleaning their hands, Koichi loses his balance, falls and cries. The caregiver turns to see him pull himself up. "Are you getting tired, Koichi? How would you like to have a drink of juice before you take your nap?" The carer takes from a high shelf a tray with a covered pitcher of diluted juice and sits on a picnic blanket. Gina, Danielle and Koichi go to her. "When you sit down, I'll pour your juice," the carer says. She pours small amounts in each glass, and the children drink and ask for more. In the adjacent room Ben continues lying on the toy shelf.

Third Stop – Toddler Room

Our last stop is in the young toddler room, where Kisha is standing in front of a shelf displaying an assortment of hats and caps. Visible through a very large picture window is an enclosed outdoor play yard. In the play yard Lee walks repeatedly up and down a plank placed on an incline to a platform which is about eight inches high.

Christopher picks up a basket with some plastic eggs inside. David stops his activity, reaches for the basket, pulls and gets it. Christopher cries and goes near the carer. "It looks as if you didn't like David's taking the basket. You can tell him 'No.'" "No!" Christopher says. David continues to hold the basket he took.

"Who knows where there are some baskets?" asks the caregiver. Both boys run inside, find a colander and a basket for each hand. Christopher puts eggs in both of his containers and walks around. David sits and puts the eggs from his basket into a colander, then puts each egg into his mouth and takes it out again. The original basket is ignored on the patio floor.

Kisha comes outside wearing a baseball cap from the shelf. She takes it off and holds it out to the carer, who asks, "Is that for me?" The carer remains seated while Kisha puts the cap on the carer's head. Both smile.

"Are you about ready for lunch?" asks the carer. Kisha takes the carer's hand and pulls her inside, and Lee follows. The toddlers stand at the gate separating the play area from the eating area, which we see has four small chairs around a low square table, with a stool for the caregiver to sit at the corner of the table. The carer gathers in a dishpan the food, plates, glasses, a pitcher of water, a carton of milk, bibs and clean washcloths, which she places inside the fenced-off eating area.

As the carer moves toward the steps beside the washbasin, the girls have already anticipated what will happen next and run there ahead of her. "Who would like to wash their hands first?" she asks. "Oh, Kisha, I see you are already waiting by the bathroom. You must want to be first." The girls in turn wash their hands and dry them with paper towels with minimal assistance from the carer.

"Would you like to eat with us?" the carer asks Christopher and David, who leave their baskets and eggs and come to the table. "Let's wash your hands first," she says and repeats the handwashing routine with them. The four children sit around the table, with the carer at the corner. "Look what we have. I'm serving five peas to Kisha, and five peas to Lee, and five peas to David, and five peas to Christopher." As they start to eat she says, "Here is some tuna for you, and you, and you, and you," and then, "And here is a fourth of a banana for each of you." David says, "More peas." The caregiver replies, "More peas, please. You have eaten all five peas. Here are five more for you." The children finish their very small servings and repeatedly ask for replacements. The adult, though doing much of the talking, listens carefully to the words of the young toddlers and observes their non-verbal communication. It is a sociable time. Lee points to her empty glass. "Would you like some more milk, Lee?" Lee nods her head, and the carer pours a small amount for her. When the children indicate they are no longer hungry, the carer gives them each a clean, wet washcloth. After washing their hands, they return to the play area one by one as they finish, while the carer sits in the gated eating area keeping the last child company.

Two of the toddlers decide to return to the eating area, where they help their caregiver clean the table. Meanwhile the other two have each taken a book and have climbed into a low-cut box where they look at the pictures, pointing, talking and turning the pages. Then the carer offers to read a book as the children wind down before going to their mats for a rest or nap.[8]

Respect and Support for Parents

The philosophy of respect demonstrated with the infants in this visit to a RIE center also extends to parents. The center respects

---

[8] After lunch and a quiet indoor play time, slightly older toddlers who can eat with more ease join their caregiver for tooth brushing before the ritual of reading books before rest time.

parents as the most important ongoing influence in the life of a child. Orientations and tours acquaint prospective parents with the center and its philosophy. Parents and infants meet for six Saturdays before a new group of four young infants begin care at the center. Potluck suppers and educational programs are offered regularly. Parents of enrolled children are encouraged to visit at any time. A quiet place is available for mothers to nurse babies. At the end of the day, parents who come to pick up their children often linger to relax and socialize with other parents and be available to their young children before returning home.

49. RIE in a Family Child Care Home

by
Catherine Coughlan

BY THE TIME I BEGAN STUDYING with Magda Gerber, I had already decided to provide child care in my home. Caring for a small group of infants in the intimate setting of a home seemed ideal for the children and their parents. Discovering RIE made me even more motivated because of its respectful approach to being with infants.

A Safe and Peaceful Environment

One of the first things I learned from Magda was the importance of creating not only a safe but also a peaceful environment for infants. With this in mind, I chose to enroll four babies who were three to four months of age. One might think that having four young children at this age with only one caregiver would be anything but safe and peaceful. My experience was just the opposite because of what I learned from RIE.

The first step was setting up an environment that was safe. (See, *Absolutely Safe!*, page 157) Because all the very young infants were at about the same developmental level, this was much easier to accomplish than if there were a significant difference in their ages. My family room, which had two sinks and easy access to the backyard, was an ideal place to care for the infants. When inside they would play on a large flannel sheet placed over the carpet with a few play objects placed nearby. (See, *Choosing Play Objects*, page 97) When out on the deck, I placed the infants on a large bedspread. Toys were put within reach but were played with less often because the infants seemed to prefer observing the things nature provided. (See, *Outdoor Living*, page 103)

As the children's developmental needs changed, the environment was adapted to meet these needs. For example, when the infants started crawling, low ramps and climbing structures were added. (See, *Equipment: What is Really Necessary?*, page 159) Low shelves for their toys allowed them to see what was available, and they would crawl to the shelves and select the toys they wanted to play with. Once the infants became toddlers, the child-proofed living room became an additional play area where they were able to satisfy their growing need for more space.

And what about providing a peaceful place for four infants? When they were young it was very seldom that all four infants were awake at the same time. The infants who were awake played while I sat nearby, quietly observing their different ways of exploring whatever they were interested in. When an infant needed a bottle or a diaper change, I was able to give one-to-one attention to the infant I was feeding or changing while the others played on the floor. If I were feeding or changing one infant when another infant became hungry or tired, I would calmly let the infant know I heard his cry and would be with him soon. Sometimes while he waited I would need to reassure him. Did he understand my words? Not in the beginning, but over time he often was comforted by my responses to his requests for help. And the infant I was feeding or changing did not get the message from me that her time was up or that we needed to hurry and finish so I could take care of someone else. By giving each infant focused one-to-one attention during caregiving times, such as feeding and diapering, I was letting the infant know how important it was for both of us to spend this kind of time together. (See, *Caregiving Routines: One-to-One, with Full Attention*, page 5 and *A Brief Visit to a RIE Infant Center*, page 193)

RIE's approach to infant play also contributed to the peacefulness of the environment. The infants were allowed to move their bodies and play with objects and equipment in their own way. No one was trying to coax the infants to crawl or walk or to teach them how to play. In other words, the infants were not expected to perform for adults. As a result I observed infants having long attention spans, experimenting endlessly and being fully self-directed. So often I would notice how an infant played with a toy in a way that many adults would not encourage and even try to correct. I remember seeing an infant dumping the soft blocks out of a container and putting the container on his head, using the lid to make a variety of movements and noises on the floor, and putting the blocks back into the container without using the holes in the lid (it is a lot more efficient). Just think of how relaxed you might feel if you were this child. I also remember noticing how the infants on a low climbing structure would each in their own way figure out how to navigate going up and down using their whole bodies for sensory input. Imagine how satisfying it would be to accomplish this on one's own without directives from adults. (See, *On Teaching and Learning*, page 11, *On Their Backs, Free to Move*, page 35 and *At Their Own Time, and In Their Own Way*, page 53)

Did the infants experience frustration? Of course, it is a natural part of play. Learning how to deal with frustration is an important part of life. Allowing infants to wrestle with their frustrations often led to creative problem solving. Once two infants were tugging back and forth on a toy, each trying to get it from the other and letting everyone know about their discontent. Rather than intervening right away, I waited to see how they might play this out. Within a short time, they began smiling at each other while continuing to tug away at the toy. They had discovered a way to play with it together and found it fun.

What about times when the infants are clearly overly frustrated during play? Then it is time to intervene and help them regain their sense of well being. RIE recommends doing the least amount of intervention first. This allows the infants to be part of the solution instead of feeling as if there is nothing they can do. For example, an infant was very frustrated because a toy he had been playing with rolled under the gate. I approached him, got down on his level and said, "I see how upset you are." Then I waited for the child's response. He reached out for me. I leaned over and held him until he released his hold on me and then went crawling off on a new adventure. Following his lead was important because what he wanted by then was comfort, not the toy.

One of the positive experiences of group care is the interaction among the infants. From the beginning the infants were interested in one another. Allowing their relationships with one another to develop provided a wealth of ongoing opportunities for learning to be with others their own age. It also enabled them to be more independent in their play while I was feeding or diapering one of them. Keeping the group size small was essential in maintaining a peaceful environment. Noise and activity levels rise and infants can easily become over-stimulated when too much is going on around them.

Predictability is another way to ensure a peaceful environment. When infants learn what to expect and do not have to adapt to frequent changes in their routine, they feel more comfortable and tend to cry less. Our daily activities were quite simple. When the infants were not sleeping, eating or having a diaper change, they were playing in the family room or out in the backyard. Whenever I wanted to do something to change what was going on, I would tell the infants what I was about to do. This included everything from letting an infant know I was going to pick her up for a diaper change to telling the group I was going to open the back door so we could go outside. Of course, in the beginning the infants did not understand my words; but over time I noticed how much more relaxed they became when making transitions compared to other infants I had observed who were not given time to anticipate change. (See, *Predictability: Helping Your Child Feel Secure*, page 57)

Parent Relations

Because the program I was offering was based on a specific approach to child care, I felt it was very important to explain the basic principles of RIE to the parents who wanted to enroll their infants. It was essential for the parents to feel that the RIE approach was what they wanted for their child. I was very grateful that Magda kept reminding me of this when I would call her to discuss what was happening during the enrollment period.

During the initial interview with each set of parents, we watched the RIE video *Seeing Infants with New Eyes* together. We talked about the kind of care their child would be receiving, and I responded to the many questions they asked. Providing them with printed materials about RIE and information about my background and training was also very helpful. Once I started enrolling infants, the parents were able to observe the program in action as well as hear about it during our interview.

During the process of enrolling the four infants, it was

obvious that the RIE approach was not a match for some parents. Validating the parents' choice was very important to them and to me. However, it did not take long to be fully enrolled. I found that the gradual enrollment of the infants helped all of us ease into the daily routine of being together.

In addition to talking with parents about their infants at drop-off and pick-up times, I also wrote daily written reports about their child's day, including eating, diapering and sleeping information as well as a comment about something that made that day special for their child. Whenever a parent requested time to discuss something in more detail, we made arrangements to do so at a time convenient for both of us.

Every month I wrote a newsletter for the parents. It included child development articles as well as calendar updates and information about what was going on in the program.

Building a Sense of Community

Two months after the fourth child was enrolled, all the parents and their infants gathered in my home for our first annual Holiday Party. I still remember the parents saying how wonderful it was to be at a holiday gathering with their infants in a place that was child-proof and child-friendly. They could relax and enjoy the party while their children played freely in a safe and fun environment.

As a result of the success of the party, we began having potluck get-togethers as an extended family every few months. Eventually we started meeting at the families' homes and then at local parks. Often questions about child care and child development would come up, and we would discuss them in a relaxed and informal way.

Grandparents became a very important part of our family

child care community. Some lived near my home and often stopped by during drop-off or pick-up times. Those who lived far away were always invited to spend time with their grandchild during their visits. I felt it was very important for grandparents to observe and feel welcome. For the most part, the grandparents had never used child care, and they needed to see what their grandchildren experienced during the day.

From Infancy to Preschool Age

I decided to enroll two additional toddlers when the original group members were two years old. The newcomers were just a few months younger and developmentally were at about the same level. Because of the increased size of the group, I also hired a part-time assistant who was willing to be trained in the RIE approach and quickly demonstrated his ability to translate theory into practice.

My original plan was to take care of these children until they were about three years old when they would be old enough to attend preschool. I was then going to enroll a new group of infants. Life presented different opportunities, however. The parents wanted their children to stay in my family child care setting; several children remained until they were five years old.

Observing the children throughout their preschool years, I could see how RIE influenced their growth and development. One time my experience of this was confirmed by a parent interested in enrolling his preschool child. After watching the children at play for about an hour, he commented that he had never before seen preschoolers playing so creatively. He marveled at how they initiated complex ways of enhancing their play without adult prompting. I explained that from a very early age the children had developed these skills simply by not having adults interfere with their play. Adults intervened only when necessary, thereby allowing the children to use their imaginations individually and as a group.

Lessons Learned

The children in the program continually demonstrated the benefits of RIE's respectful approach to infant care. The following are some of the experiences I would like to share.

I learned firsthand the importance of infants in child care being in a small group with a primary caregiver. Focusing on only four infants, I was able to recognize their subtle cues and respond to their needs in ways which helped them to develop trust in me and confidence in their ability to communicate. I could also see how comforting this was for them.

RIE's emphasis on talking with infants as if they understand led to many interesting results. (See, *Talking to Your Baby*, page 33) One example involves a toddler who had been in the program only one week. Prior to being enrolled, he had not heard the English language. One day when we were on the deck and the children were engaged in water play, I mentioned that I had forgotten to bring out the sponges. He immediately went into the house, opened the cabinet where the sponges were kept and brought them out for the group. His matter-of-fact way of doing this was particularly amazing.

Treating others as you have been treated was brought home to me when I observed an older sibling interacting with her younger brother. Once when he was throwing a toy, she gently told him it was not safe and showed him a way he could throw it that was safe. He was intrigued and immediately began throwing the toy as she had demonstrated. She was only three, and she already knew how to redirect inappropriate behavior.

The five years of providing child care in my home are among the most treasured of my life. After closing the program when the oldest children entered kindergarten, I felt the lessons I had learned from the child care experience provided a solid foundation for my subsequent work teaching others about RIE.

Index

Order Form

Please send me:

__ copies of **DEAR PARENT** ($15.95+$3 shipping=$18.95)
(California residents add $1.32 for sales tax = $20.27)

Name _____

Address _____

City _____ State _____ Zip _____

Telephone (____) _____
Payment: ❐   Check
           ❐   Visa, ❐ Master Card – Exp. Date _____
           ❐   I would like to support RIE as a general member ($40
               per year) and receive quarterly issues of *Educaring*.

Card Number _____

Name on card _____

Signature _____

Send this form (and check, if applicable) to:
RESOURCES FOR INFANT EDUCARERS
1550 Murray Circle
Los Angeles, CA 90026

Fax orders: (323) 663-5586
Telephone orders: (323) 663-5330
Web page order: www.RIE.org